W9-CBR-967

DATE DUE

FEB 0 1 1999			
APR 2 9 1999			

Inc. 38-293

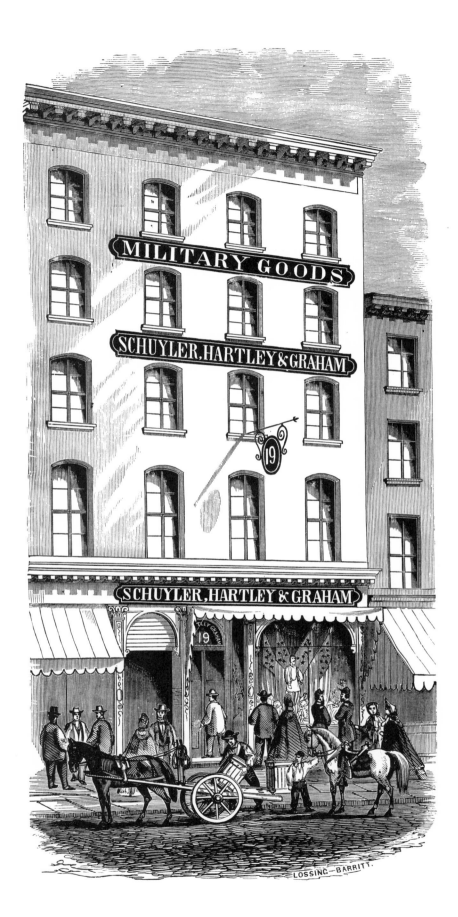

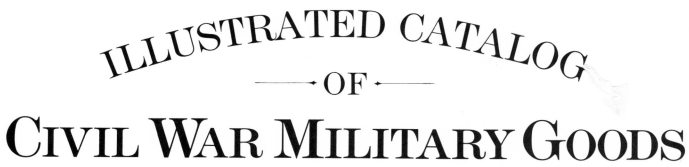

ILLUSTRATED CATALOG
· OF ·
CIVIL WAR MILITARY GOODS

Union Weapons, Insignia, Uniform Accessories and Other Equipment

· BY ·

SCHUYLER, HARTLEY & GRAHAM

DOVER PUBLICATIONS, INC.
NEW YORK

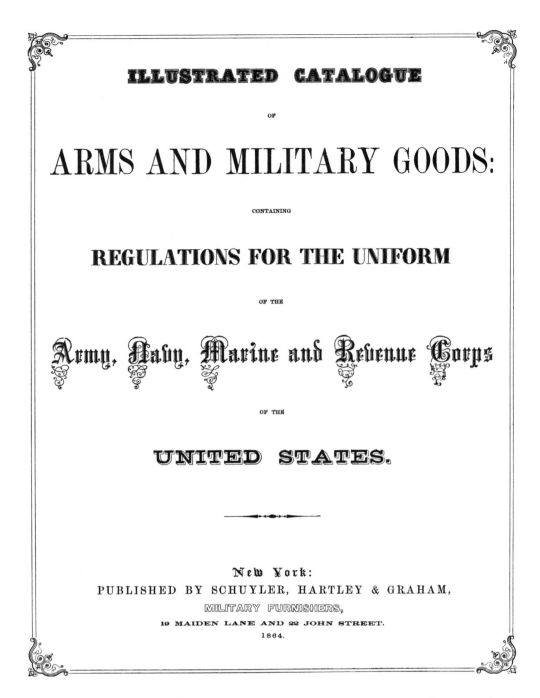

ILLUSTRATED CATALOGUE

OF

ARMS AND MILITARY GOODS:

CONTAINING

REGULATIONS FOR THE UNIFORM

OF THE

Army, Navy, Marine and Revenue Corps

OF THE

UNITED STATES.

New York:
PUBLISHED BY SCHUYLER, HARTLEY & GRAHAM,
MILITARY FURNISHERS,
19 MAIDEN LANE AND 22 JOHN STREET.
1864.

Published in Canada by General Publishing Company, Ltd., 30 Lesmill Road, Don Mills, Toronto, Ontario.
Published in the United Kingdom by Constable and Company, Ltd.

This Dover edition, first published in 1985, is an unabridged, slightly altered republication of the work first published by Schuyler, Hartley & Graham, New York, in 1864 under the title *Illustrated Catalogue of Arms and Military Goods: Containing Regulations for the Uniform of the Army, Navy, Marine and Revenue Corps of the United States.* The eight plates that appeared in color in the original edition are reproduced in black and white in the present edition, on pages 2, 80B and 96A–F.

DOVER *Pictorial Archive* SERIES

Manufactured in the United States of America
Dover Publications, Inc., 31 East 2nd Street, Mineola, N.Y. 11501

Library of Congress Cataloging-in-Publication Data

Schuyler, Hartley & Graham.
  Illustrated catalog of Civil War military goods.

  Rev. ed. of: Illustrated catalogue of arms and military goods. 1864.
  1. United States—History—Civil War, 1861–1865—Collectibles—Catalogs. 2. Schuyler, Hartley & Graham—Catalogs. I. Schuyler, Hartley & Graham. Illustrated catalog of arms and military goods. II. Title.
E646.5.S38   1985   973.7   85-6819
ISBN 0-486-24939-5

CONTENTS.

	PAGE.
ARMY UNIFORM DRESS AND HORSE EQUIPMENTS,	5–20
FLAGS AND GUIDONS,	20, 21
ARMY PAY ROLL,	22–25
ARMY ILLUSTRATIONS,	29–80
NAVY UNIFORM,	81–86
NAVY PAY ROLL,	87–90
ORGANIZATION OF NAVY DEPARTMENT,	91, 92
NAVY ILLUSTRATIONS,	95–103
MASONIC GOODS,	104, 105
MARINE CORPS UNIFORM,	109–120
REVENUE UNIFORM,	123, 124
ARMS AND AMMUNITION,	127–142
COATS OF ARMS,	143–146

REGULATIONS

FOR THE

Uniform and Dress

OF

THE ARMY

Of the United States.

SCHUYLER, HARTLEY & GRAHAM'S

ILLUSTRATED

Catalogue of Military Goods.

Uniform, Dress and Horse Equipments.

COAT.

For Commissioned Officers.

1. All officers shall wear a frock-coat of dark blue cloth, the skirt to extend from two-thirds to three-fourths of the distance from the top of the hip to the bend of the knee; single-breasted for Captains and Lieutenants; double-breasted for all other grades.

2. *For a Major-General*—two rows of buttons on the breast, nine in each row, placed by threes; the distance between each row, five and one-half inches at top, and three and one-half inches at bottom; stand-up collar, to rise no higher than to permit the chin to turn freely over it, to hook in front at the bottom, and slope thence up and backward at an angle of thirty degrees on each side; cuffs two and one-half inches deep, to go around the sleeves parallel with the lower edge, and to button with three small buttons at the under seam; pockets in the folds of the skirts, with one button at the hip, and one at the end of each pocket, making four buttons on the back and skirt of the coat, the hip button to range with the lowest buttons on the breast; collar and cuffs to be of dark blue velvet; lining of the coat, black.

3. *For a Brigadier-General*—the same as for a Major-General, except that there will be only eight buttons in each row on the breast, placed in pairs.

4. *For a Colonel*—the same as for a Major-General, except that there will be only seven buttons in each row on the breast, placed at equal distances; collar and cuffs of the same color and material as the coat.

5. *For a Lieutenant-Colonel*—the same as for a Colonel.

6. *For a Major*—the same as for a Colonel.

7. *For a Captain*—the same as for a Colonel, except that there will be only one row of nine buttons on the breast, placed at equal distances.

8. *For a First Lieutenant*—the same as for a Captain.

9. *For a Second Lieutenant*—the same as for a Captain.

10. *For a Brevet Second Lieutenant*—the same as for a Captain.

11. *For a Medical Cadet*—the same as for a Brevet Second Lieutenant.

12. A round jacket, according to pattern, of dark blue cloth, trimmed with scarlet, with the Russian shoulder-knot, the prescribed insignia of rank to be worked in silver in the centre of the knot, may be worn on undress duty by officers of Light Artillery.

For Enlisted Men.

13. The uniform coat for all enlisted *foot* men shall be a single-breasted frock, of dark blue cloth, made without plaits, with a skirt extending one-half the distance from the top of the hip to the bend of the knee; one row of nine buttons on the breast, placed at equal distances; stand-up collar, to rise no higher than to permit the chin to turn freely over it, to hook in front at the bottom, and then to slope up and backward at an angle of thirty degrees on each side; cuffs pointed according to pattern, and to button with two small buttons at the under seam; collar and cuffs edged with a cord or welt of cloth as follows, to wit: Scarlet *for Artillery;* sky-blue *for Infantry;* yellow *for Engineers;* crimson *for Ordnance* and *Hospital Stewards.* On each shoulder a metallic scale according to pattern; narrow lining for skirt of the coat, of the same color and material as the coat; pockets in the folds of the skirts, with one button at each hip to range with the lowest buttons on the breast; no buttons at the ends of the pockets.

14. *All Enlisted Men of the Cavalry and Light Artillery* shall wear a uniform jacket of dark blue cloth, with one row of twelve small buttons on the breast, placed at equal distances; stand-up collar, to rise no higher than to permit the chin to turn freely over it, to hook in front at the bottom, and to slope the same as the coat collar; on the collar, on each side, two blind button-holes of lace, three-eighths of an inch wide, one small button on the button-hole, lower button-hole extending back four inches, upper button-hole three and a half inches; top button and front ends of collar bound with lace, three-eighths of an inch wide, and a strip of the same extending down the front and around the whole lower edge of the jacket; the back seam laced with the same, and on the cuff a point of the same shape as that on the coat, but formed of the lace; jacket to extend to the waist, and to be lined with white flannel; two small buttons at the under seam of the cuff, as on the coat cuff; one hook and eye at the bottom of the collar; color of lace (worsted), yellow for *Cavalry,* and scarlet for *Light Artillery.*

15. *For all Musicians*—the same as for other enlisted men of their respective corps, with the addition of a facing of lace, three-eighths of an inch wide, on the front of the *coat or jacket,* made in the following manner: bars of three-eighths of an inch worsted lace placed on a line with each button, six and one-half inches wide at the bottom, and *thence* gradually expanding upward to the last button, counting from the waist up, and contracting from thence to the bottom of the collar, where it will be six and one-half inches wide, with a strip of the same lace following the bars at their outer extremity—the whole presenting something of what is called the herring-bone form; the color of the lace facing to correspond with the color of the trimming of the corps.

16. *For Fatigue Purposes*—a sack coat of dark blue flannel, extending half-way down the thigh, and made loose, without sleeve or body lining, falling collar, inside pocket on the left side, four coat buttons down the front.

17. *For Recruits*—the sack coat will be made with sleeve and body lining, the latter of flannel.

18. On all occasions of duty, except fatigue, and when out of quarters, the coat or jacket shall be buttoned and hooked at the collar.

BUTTONS.

19. *For General Officers and Officers of the General Staff*—gilt, convex, with spread eagle and stars, and plain border; large size, seven-eighths of an inch in exterior diameter; small size, one-half inch.

20. *For Officers of the Corps of Engineers*—gilt, nine-tenths of an inch in exterior diameter, slightly convex; a raised bright rim, one thirtieth of an inch wide; device, an eagle holding in his beak a scroll, with the word "*Essayons*," a bastion with embrasures in the distance surrounded by water, with a rising sun—the figures to be of dead gold upon a bright field. Small buttons of the same form and device, and fifty-five hundredths of an inch in exterior diameter.

21. *For Officers of the Corps of Topographical Engineers*—gilt, seven-eighths of an inch exterior diameter, convex and solid; device, the shield of the United States, occupying one-half the diameter, and the letters 𝔗. 𝔈., in old English characters, the other half; small buttons, one-half inch diameter, device and form the same.

22. *For Officers of the Ordnance Department*—gilt, convex, plain border, cross cannon and bomb-shell, with a circular scroll over and across the cannon, containing the words "Ordnance Corps;" large size, seven-eighths of an inch in exterior diameter; small size, one-half inch.

23. *For Officers of Artillery, Infantry and Cavalry*—gilt, convex, device, a spread eagle, with the letter A, for Artillery—I, for Infantry—C, for Cavalry, on the shield; large size, seven-eighths of an inch in exterior diameter; small size, one-half inch.

24. *Aides-de-camp* may wear the button of the General Staff, or of their regiment or corps, at their option.

25. *For Medical Cadets*—same as for Officers of the General Staff.

26. *For all Enlisted Men*—yellow, the same as is used by the Artillery, &c., omitting the letter in the shield.

TROWSERS.

27. *For General Officers and Officers of the Ordnance Department*—of dark blue cloth, plain, without stripe, welt or cord, down the outer seam.

28. *For Officers of the General Staff and Staff Corps*, except the Ordnance—dark blue cloth, with a gold cord, one-eighth of an inch in diameter, along the outer seam.

29. *For all Regimental Officers*—dark blue cloth, with a welt let into the outer seam, one-eighth of an inch in diameter, of colors corresponding to the facings of the respective regiments, viz.: *Cavalry*, yellow; *Artillery*, scarlet; *Infantry*, sky-blue.

30. *For Medical Cadets*—same as for Officers of the General Staff, except a welt of buff cloth, instead of a gold cord.

31 *For Enlisted Men*, except companies of Light Artillery—dark blue cloth; *Sergeants*, with a stripe one and one-half inch wide; *Corporals*, with a stripe one-half inch wide, of worsted lace, down and over the outer seam, of the color of the facings of the respective corps.

32. *Ordnance Sergeants and Hospital Stewards*—stripe of crimson lace, one and one-half inch wide.

33. *Privates*—plain, without stripe or welt.

34. *For Companies of Artillery equipped as Light Artillery*—sky-blue cloth.

All trowsers to be made loose, without plaits, and to spread well over the boot; to be re-enforced for all enlisted mounted men.

HAT.

35. *For Officers*—of best black felt.   The dimensions of medium size to be as follows:

Width of brim, $3\frac{1}{4}$ inches.

Height of crown, $6\frac{1}{4}$ inches.

Oval of tip, $\frac{1}{2}$ inch.

Taper of crown, $\frac{3}{4}$ inch.

Curve of head, $\frac{3}{8}$ inch.

36. *For Enlisted Men*—of black felt, same shape and size as for officers, with double row of stitching, instead of binding, around the edge.   To agree in quality with the pattern deposited in the clothing arsenal.

37. *Medical Cadets* will wear a forage cap according to pattern.

Trimmings.

38. *For General Officers*—gold cord, with acorn-shaped ends.   The brim of the hat looped up on the right side, and fastened with an eagle attached to the side of the hat; three black ostrich-feathers on the left side; a gold-embroidered wreath in front, on black velvet ground, encircling the letters U. S., in silver, old English characters.

39. *For Officers of the Adjutant-General's, Inspector-General's, Quartermaster's, Subsistence, Medical and Pay Departments, and the Judge-Advocate, above the rank of Captain*—the same as for General Officers, except the cord, which will be of black silk and gold.

40. *For the same Departments, below the rank of Field Officers*—the same as for Field Officers, except that there will be but two feathers.

41. *For Officers of the Corps of Engineers*—The same as for the General Staff, except the ornament in front, which will be a gold-embroidered wreath of laurel and palm, encircling a silver turreted castle, on black velvet ground.

42. *For Officers of the Topographical Engineers*—the same as for the General Staff, except the ornament in front, which will be a gold-embroidered wreath of oak leaves, encircling a gold-embroidered shield, on black velvet ground.

43. *For Officers of the Ordnance Department*—the same as for the General Staff, except the ornament in front, which will be a gold-embroidered shell and flame, on black velvet ground.

44. *For Officers of Cavalry*—the same as for the General Staff, except the ornament in front, which will be two gold-embroidered sabres crossed, edges upward, on black velvet ground, with the number of the regiment, in silver, in the upper angle.

45. *For Officers of Artillery*—the same as for the General Staff, except the ornament in front, which will be gold-embroidered cross-cannon, on black velvet ground, with the number of the regiment in silver at the intersection of the cross-cannon.

46. *For Officers of Infantry*—the same as for Artillery, except the ornament in front, which will be a gold-embroidered bugle, on black velvet ground, with the number of the regiment in silver within the bend.

47. *For Enlisted Men*, except companies of Light Artillery—the same as for officers of the respective corps, except that there will be but one feather, the cord will be of worsted, of the same color as that of the facing of the corps, three-sixteenths of an inch in diameter, running three times through a slide of the same material, and terminating with two tassels, not less than two inches long, on the side of the hat opposite the feather. The insignia of corps, in brass, in front of the hat, corresponding with those prescribed for officers, with the number of regiment, five-eighths of an inch long, in brass, and letter of company, one inch, in brass, arranged over insignia.

48. *For Hospital Stewards* the cord will be of buff and green mixed. The wreath in front of brass, with the letters U. S. in Roman, of white metal. Brim to be looped up to side of hat with a brass eagle, having a hook attached to the bottom to secure the brim—on the right side for mounted men and left side for foot men. The feather to be worn on the side opposite the loop.

49. All the trimmings of the hat are to be made so that they can be detached; but the eagle, badge of corps, and letter of company, are to be always worn.

50. For companies of Artillery, equipped as Light Artillery, the old pattern uniform cap, with red horsehair plume, cord and tassel.

51. Officers of the General Staff, and Staff Corps, may wear, at their option, a light French chapeau, either stiff crown or flat, according to the pattern deposited in the Adjutant-General's office. Officers below the rank of field officers to wear but two feathers.

FORAGE CAPS.

52. For fatigue purposes, forage caps, of pattern in the Quartermaster-General's office: dark blue cloth, with a welt of the same around the crown, and yellow metal letters in front to designate companies.

53. Commissioned officers may wear forage caps of the same pattern, with the distinctive ornament of the corps and regiment in front.

CRAVAT OR STOCK.

54. *For all Officers*—black; when a cravat is worn, the tie not to be visible at the opening of the collar.

55. *For all Enlisted Men*—black leather, according to pattern.

BOOTS.

56. *For all Officers*—ankle or Jefferson.

57. *For Enlisted Men of Cavalry and Light Artillery*—ankle and Jefferson, rights and lefts, according to pattern.

58. *For Enlisted Men of Artillery, Infantry, Engineers, and Ordnance*—Jefferson, rights and lefts, according to pattern.

SPURS.

59. *For all Mounted Officers*—yellow metal, or gilt.

60. *For all Enlisted Mounted Men*—yellow metal, according to pattern (See par. 179.)

GLOVES.

61. *For General Officers and Officers of the General Staff and Staff Corps*—buff or white.

62. *For Officers of Artillery, Infantry, Cavalry, Dragoons, and Riflemen*—white.

SASH.

63. *For General Officers*—buff, silk net, with silk bullion fringe ends; sash to go twice around the waist, and to tie behind the left hip, pendent part not to extend more than eighteen inches below the tie.

64. *For Officers of the Adjutant-General's, Inspector-General's, Quartermaster's, and Subsistence Departments, Corps of Engineers, Topographical Engineers, Ordnance, Artillery, Infantry, Cavalry, and the Judge-Advocate of the Army*—crimson silk net; *for Officers of the Medical Department*—medium or emerald green silk net, with silk bullion fringe ends; to go around the waist, and tie as for General Officers.

65. *For all Sergeant Majors, Quartermaster Sergeants, Ordnance Sergeants, Hospital Stewards, First Sergeants, Principal or Chief Musicians and Chief Buglers*—red worsted sash, with worsted bullion fringe ends; to go twice around the waist, and to tie behind the left hip, pendent part not to extend more than eighteen inches below the tie.

66. The sash will be worn (over the coat) on all occasions of duty of every description, except stable and fatigue.

67. The sash will be worn by "*Officers of the Day*," across the body, scarf fashion, from the right shoulder to the left side, instead of around the waist, tying behind the left hip as prescribed.

SWORD-BELT.

68. *For all Officers*—a waist-belt not less than one and one-half inch nor more than two inches wide; to be worn over the sash; the sword to be suspended from it by slings, of the same material as the belt, with a hook attached to the belt, upon which the sword may be hung.

69. *For General Officers*—Russia leather, with three stripes of gold embroidery; the slings embroidered on both sides.

70. *For all other Officers*—black leather, plain.

71. *For all Non-commissioned Officers*—black leather, plain.

SWORD-BELT PLATE.

72. *For all Officers and Enlisted Men*—gilt, rectangular, two inches wide, with a raised bright rim; a silver wreath of laurel encircling the "Arms of the United States;" eagle, shield, scroll, edge of cloud

and rays bright. The motto, "E PLURIBUS UNUM," in silver letters, upon the scroll; stars also of silver; according to pattern.

SWORD AND SCABBARD.

73. *For General Officers*—straight sword, gilt hilt, silver grip, brass or steel scabbard.

74. *For Officers of the Adjutant-General's, Inspector-General's, Quartermaster's, and Subsistence Departments, Corps of Engineers, Topographical Engineers, Ordnance, the Judge-Advocate of the Army, Aides-de-Camp, Field Officers of Artillery, Infantry and Foot Riflemen, and for the Light Artillery*—the sword of the pattern adopted by the War Department, April 9, 1850; or the one described in General Orders No. 21, of August 28, 1860, for officers therein designated.

75. *For the Medical and Pay Departments*—small sword and scabbard, according to pattern in the Surgeon-General's office.

76. *For Medical Cadets*—the sword and belt and plate will be the same as for non-commissioned officers.

77. *For Officers of Cavalry*—sabre and scabbard now in use, according to pattern in the Ordnance Department.

78. *For the Artillery, Infantry, and Foot Riflemen*, except the field officers—the sword of the pattern adopted by the War Department, April 9, 1850.

79. The sword and sword-belt will be worn upon all occasions of duty, without exception.

80. When on foot, the sabre will be suspended from the hook attached to the belt.

81. When not on military duty, officers may wear swords of honor, or the prescribed sword, with a scabbard, gilt, or of leather with gilt mountings.

SWORD-KNOT.

82. *For General Officers*—gold cord with acorn end.

83. *For all other Officers*—gold lace strap with gold bullion tassel.

BADGES TO DISTINGUISH RANK.

Epaulettes.

84. *For the Major-General Commanding the Army*—gold, with solid crescent; device, three silver-embroidered stars, one, one and a half inches in diameter, one, one and one-fourth inches in diameter, and one, one and one-eighth inches in diameter, placed on the strap in a row, longitudinally, and equidistant, the largest star in the centre of the crescent, the smallest at the top; dead and bright gold bullion; one-half inch in diameter and three and one-half inches long.

85. *For all other Major-Generals*—the same as for the Major-General Commanding the Army, except that there will be two stars on the strap instead of three, omitting the smallest.

86. *For a Brigadier-General*—the same as for a Major-General, except that, instead of two, there shall be one star (omitting the smallest) placed upon the strap, and not within the crescent.

87. *For a Colonel*—the same as for a Brigadier-General, substituting a silver-embroidered spread eagle for the star upon the strap; and within the crescent for the *Medical Department*—a laurel wreath embroidered in gold, and the letters 𝔐. 𝔖., in old English characters, in silver, within the wreath; *Pay*

Department—same as the Medical Department, with the letters 𝔓. 𝔇., in old English characters; *Corps of Engineers*—a turreted castle of silver; *Corps of Topographical Engineers*—a shield embroidered in gold, and below it the letters 𝔗. 𝔈., in old English characters; in silver; *Ordnance Department*—shell and flame in silver embroidery; *Regimental Officers*—the number of the regiment embroidered in gold, within a circlet of embroidered silver, one and three-fourths inches in diameter, upon cloth of the following colors: *for Artillery*—scarlet; *Infantry*—light or sky blue; *Cavalry*—yellow.

88. *For Lieutenant-Colonel*—the same as for a Colonel, according to corps, but substituting for the eagle a silver-embroidered leaf.

89. *For a Major*—the same as for a Colonel, according to corps, omitting the eagle.

90. *For a Captain*—the same as for a Colonel, according to corps, except that the bullion will be only one-fourth of an inch in diameter, and two and one-half inches long, and substituting for the eagle two silver embroidered bars.

91. *For a First Lieutenant*—the same as for a Colonel, according to corps, except that the bullion will be only one-eighth of an inch in diameter, and two and one-half inches long, and substituting for the eagle one silver-embroidered bar.

92. *For a Second Lieutenant*—the same as for a First Lieutenant, omitting the bar.

93. *For a Brevet Second Lieutenant*—the same as for a Second Lieutenant.

94. All officers having military rank will wear an epaulette on each shoulder.

95. The epaulette may be dispensed with when not on duty, and on certain duties off parade, to wit: at drills, at inspections of barracks and hospitals, on Courts of Inquiry and Boards, at inspections of articles and necessaries, on working parties and fatigue duties, and upon the march, except when, in war, there is immediate expectation of meeting the enemy, and also when the overcoat is worn.

Shoulder Straps.

96. *For the Major-General Commanding the Army*—dark blue cloth, one and three-eighths inches wide by four inches long; bordered with an embroidery of gold one-fourth of an inch wide; three silver-embroidered stars of five rays, one star on the centre of the strap, and one on each side equidistant between the centre and the outer edge of the strap; the centre star to be the largest.

97. *For all other Major-Generals*—the same as for the Major-General Commanding the Army, except that there will be two stars instead of three; the center of each star to be one inch from the outer edge of the gold embroidery on the ends of the strap; both stars of the same size.

98. *For a Brigadier-General*—the same as for a Major-General, except that there will be one star instead of two; the centre of the star to be equidistant from the outer edge of the embroidery on the ends of the strap.

99. *For a Colonel*—the same size as for a Major-General, and bordered in like manner with an embroidery of gold; a silver-embroidered spread eagle on the centre of the strap, two inches between the tips of the wings, having in the right talon an olive-branch, and in the left a bundle of arrows; an escutcheon on the breast, as represented in the arms of the United States; cloth of the strap as follows: for the *General Staff and Staff Corps*—dark blue; *Artillery*—scarlet; *Infantry*—light or sky blue; *Cavalry*—yellow.

100. *For a Lieutenant-Colonel*—the same as for a Colonel, according to corps, omitting the eagle, and

introducing a silver-embroidered leaf at each end, each leaf extending seven-eighths of an inch from the end border of the strap.

101. *For a Major*—the same as for a Colonel, according to corps, omitting the eagle, and introducing a gold-embroidered leaf at each end, each leaf extending seven-eighths of an inch from the end border of the strap.

102. *For a Captain*—the same as for a Colonel, according to corps, omitting the eagle, and introducing at each end two gold-embroidered bars of the same width as the border, placed parallel to the ends of the strap; the distance between them and from the border equal to the width of the border.

103. *For a First Lieutenant*—the same as for a Colonel, according to corps, omitting the eagle, and introducing at each end one gold-embroidered bar of the same width as the border, placed parallel to the ends of the strap, at a distance from the border equal to its width.

104. *For a Second Lieutenant*—the same as for a Colonel, according to corps, omitting the eagle.

105. *For a Brevet Second Lieutenant*—the same as for a Second Lieutenant.

106. *For a Medical Cadet*—a strip of gold lace three inches long, half an inch wide, placed in the middle of a strap of green cloth three and three-quarter inches long by one and one-quarter inches wide.

107. The shoulder-strap will be worn whenever the epaulette is not.

Chevrons.

108. The rank of non-commissioned officers will be marked by chevrons upon both sleeves of the uniform coat and overcoat, above the elbow, of silk or worsted binding one-half an inch wide, same color as the edging on the coat, points down, as follows:

109. *For a Sergeant-Major*—three bars and an arc, in silk.

110. *For a Quartermaster Sergeant*—three bars and a tie, in silk.

111. *For an Ordnance Sergeant*—three bars and a star, in silk.

112. *For a Hospital Steward*—a half chevron of the following description—viz.: of emerald green cloth, one and three-fourths inches wide, running obliquely downward from the outer to the inner seam of the sleeve, and at an angle of about thirty degrees with a horizontal, parallel to, and one-eighth of an inch distant from, both the upper and lower edge, an embroidery of yellow silk one-eighth of an inch wide, and in the centre a "caduceus" two inches long, embroidered also with yellow silk, the head toward the outer seam of the sleeve.

113. *For a First Sergeant*—three bars and a lozenge, in worsted.

114. *For a Sergeant*—three bars, in worsted.

115. *For a Corporal*—two bars, in worsted.

116. *For a Pioneer*—two crossed hatchets of cloth, same color and material as the edging of the collar, to be sewed on each arm above the elbow in the place indicated for a chevron (those of a corporal to be just above and resting on the chevron), the head of the hatchet upward, its edge outward, of the following dimensions, viz.: *Handle*—four and one-half inches long, one-fourth to one-third of an inch wide. *Hatchet*—two inches long, one inch wide at the edge.

117. *To indicate service*—all non-commissioned officers, musicians, and privates, who have served faithfully for the term of five years, will wear, as a mark of distinction, upon both sleeves of the uniform coat, below the elbow, a diagonal half chevron, one-half an inch wide, extending from seam to seam, the

front end nearest the cuff, and one-half an inch above the point of the cuff, to be of the same color as the edging on the coat.   In like manner, an additional half chevron, above and parallel to the first, for every subsequent five years of faithful service; distance between each chevron one-fourth of an inch.   Service in war will be indicated by a light or sky blue stripe on each side of the chevron for Artillery, and a red stripe for all other corps, the stripe to be one-eighth of an inch wide.

OVERCOAT.

For Commissioned Officers.

118. A "*cloak coat*" of dark blue cloth, closing by means of four frog buttons of black silk and loops of black silk cord down the breast, and at the throat by a long loop *à échelle*, without tassel or plate, on the left side, and a black silk frog button on the right; cord for the loops fifteen-hundredths of an inch in diameter; back, a single piece, slit up from the bottom, from fifteen to seventeen inches, according to the height of the wearer, and closing at will, by buttons, and button-holes cut in a concealed flap; collar of the same color and material as the coat, rounded at the edges, and to stand or fall; when standing, to be about five inches high; sleeves loose, of a single piece, and round at the bottom, without cuff or slit; lining, woolen; around the front and lower border, the edges of the pockets, the edges of the sleeves, collar, and slit in the back, a flat braid of black silk one-half an inch wide; and around each frog button on the breast, a knot two and one-quarter inches in diameter of black silk cord, seven-hundredths of an inch in diameter, arranged according to drawing; cape of the same color and material as the coat, removable at the pleasure of the wearer, and reaching to the cuff of the coat-sleeve when the arm is extended; coat to extend down the leg from six to eight inches below the knee, according to height.   *To indicate rank,* there will be on both sleeves, near the lower edge, a knot of flat black silk braid not exceeding one-eighth of an inch in width, arranged according to drawing, and composed as follows:

119. *For a General*—of five braids, double knot.

120. *For a Colonel*—of five braids, single knot.

121. *For a Lieutenant-Colonel*—of four braids, single knot.

122. *For a Major*—of three braids, single knot.

123. *For a Captain*—of two braids, single knot.

124. *For a First Lieutenant*—of one braid, single knot.

125. *For a Second Lieutenant and Brevet Second Lieutenant*—a plain sleeve, without knot or ornament.

For Enlisted Men.

126. *Of all Mounted Corps*—of sky-blue cloth; stand-and-fall collar; double breasted; cape to reach down to the cuff of the coat when the arm is extended, and to button all the way up; buttons (198).

127. *All other Enlisted Men*—of sky-blue cloth; stand-up collar; single-breasted; cape to reach down to the elbows when the arm is extended, and to button all the way up; buttons (198).

128. *For Cavalry*—a gutta-percha talma, or cloak extending to the knee, with long sleeves.

OTHER ARTICLES OF CLOTHING AND EQUIPMENT.

129. *Flannel shirt, drawers, stockings, and stable-frock*—the same as now furnished.

130. *Blanket*—woolen, gray, with letters U. S. in black, four inches long, in the centre; to be seven feet long, and five and a half feet wide, and to weigh five pounds.

131. *Canvas overalls for Engineer soldiers*—of white cotton; one garment to cover the whole of the body below the waist, the breast, the shoulders, and the arms; sleeves loose, to allow a free play of the arms, with narrow wristband buttoning with one button; overalls to fasten at the neck behind with two buttons, and at the waist behind with buckle and tongue.

132. *Belts of all Enlisted Men*—black leather.

133. *Cartridge-box*—according to pattern in the Ordnance Department.

134. *Drum-sling*—white webbing; to be provided with a brass drumstick carriage, according to pattern.

135. *Knapsack*—of painted canvas, according to pattern now issued by the Quartermaster's Department; the great-coat, when carried, to be neatly folded, not rolled, and covered by the outer flap of the knapsack.

136. *Haversack*—of painted canvas, with an inside sack unpainted, according to the pattern now issued by the Quartermaster's Department.

137. *Canteen*—of tin, covered with woolen cloth, of the pattern now issued by the Quartermaster's Department.

TENTS.

138. *For all Commissioned Officers*—wall tent, with a fly, pattern now issued by the Quartermaster's Department.

139. *For Hospital purposes*—pattern described in " General Orders " No. 1, of January 19, 1860.

140. *For all Enlisted Men*—Sibley's patent, according to the pattern now issued by the Quartermaster's Department, at the rate of one tent to 17 mounted or 20 foot men. Sheet-iron stoves will be issued with the tents in cold climates, or when specially ordered.

141. *For Officers' Servants and Laundresses*—small common tent, old pattern.

HORSE FURNITURE.
For General Officers and the General Staff.

142. *Housing for General Officers*—to be worn over the saddle; of dark blue cloth, trimmed with two rows of gold lace, the outer row one inch and five-eighths wide, the inner row two inches and one-fourth; to be made full, so as to cover the horse's haunches and forehands, and to bear on each flank corner the following ornaments, distinctive of rank, to wit: for the *Major-General Commanding the Army*—a gold-embroidered spread eagle and three stars; for other *Major-Generals*—a gold-embroidered spread eagle and two stars; for a *Brigadier-General*—a gold-embroidered spread eagle and one star.

143. *Saddle-cloth for General Staff Officers*—dark blue cloth, of sufficient length to cover the saddle and holsters, and one foot ten inches in depth, with an edging of gold lace one inch wide.

144. *Surcingle*—blue web.

145. *Bridle*—black leather; bent branch bit, with gilt bosses; the front and roses yellow.

146. *Collar*—yellow.

147. *Holsters*—black leather, with gilt mountings.

148. *Stirrups*—gilt or yellow metal.

For Officers of the Corps of Engineers and Topographical Engineers.

149. The same as for General Staff Officers.

150. In time of actual field service, General Officers and Officers of the General Staff and Staff Corps are permitted to use the horse equipments described for mounted service.

HORSE EQUIPMENTS FOR THE MOUNTED SERVICE.

151. A complete set of horse equipments for mounted troops consists of 1 *bridle*, 1 *watering bridle*, 1 *halter*, 1 *saddle*, 1 *pair saddle bags*, 1 *saddle blanket*, 1 *surcingle*, 1 *pair spurs*, 1 *currycomb*, 1 *horse brush*, 1 *picket pin*, *and* 1 *lariat ;* 1 link and 1 nose bag when specially required.

Head Gear.

152. All the *leather* is black bridle-leather, and the buckles are malleable iron, flat, bar buckles, blued.

153. BRIDLE—It is composed of 1 *headstall*, 1 *bit*, 1 *pair of reins*.

154. HEADSTALL—1 *crown piece*, the ends split, forming 1 *cheek strap* and 1 *throat lash billet* on one side, and on the other, 1 *cheek strap* and 1 *throat lash*, with 1 *buckle*, ·625 inch, 2 *chapes* and 2 *buckles* ·75 inch, sewed to the ends of cheek piece to attach the bit; 1 *brow band*, the ends doubled and sewed form 2 loops on each end through which the cheek straps and throat lash and throat lash billet pass.

155. BIT (shear steel, blued)—2 *branches*, S shaped, pierced at top with an *eye* for the cheek strap billet, and with a small hole near the eye for the curb chain, terminated at the bottom by 2 *buttons*, into which are wedded 2 *rings*, 1 inch, for the reins; 1 *mouth piece*, curved in the middle, its ends pass through the branches and are riveted to them; 1 *cross bar*, riveted to the branches near the lower ends; 2 *bosses* (cast brass), bearing the number and letter of the regiment and the letter of the company, riveted to the branches with 4 *rivets ;* 1 *curb-chain hook*, steel wire, No. 10, fastened to the *near* branch; 1 *curb chain*, steel wire, No. 11, curb-chain links 0·7 inch wide, with 1 loose ring in the middle, fastened to the *off* branch by a S hook, coldshut; 1 *curb strap* (leather), fastened to the curb chain by 2 *standing loops*.

156. 1 *curb ring* for bit No. 1 replaces the curb chain and curb strap. They are of two sizes: No. 1 has an interior diameter of 4 inches; No. 2, of 3·75 inches. The number is marked on the outside of the swell. No. 1 is the larger size.

157. There are four bits, differing from each other in the arch of the mouth piece, and in the distance from the mouth piece to the eye for the cheek strap. The branches are alike below the mouth piece. No. 1 is a Spanish bit, No. 2 is the next severest, and No. 4 is the mildest. Height of arch is $2\frac{1}{2}$ inches in No. 1, 2 inches in No. 2, $1\frac{1}{2}$ inch in No. 3, and $\frac{1}{2}$ inch in No. 4. The distance between the branches is 4·5 inches in all the bits.

158. REINS—2 *reins* sewed together at one end, the other ends sewed to the rings of the bit.

Watering Bridle.

159. The watering bridle is composed of 1 *bit* and 1 *pair of reins*.

160. BIT (wrought iron, blued)—2 *mouth-piece sides* united in the middle by a loop hinge; their ends are pierced with 2 holes to receive 2 *rings* 1·7 inches diameter for the reins. 2 *chains and toggles*, 3 links, each 1 inch × 0·55 inch, welded in the rein rings.

161. REINS—2 *reins* sewed together at one end, the other end sewed to rings of the bit.

Halter.

162. 2 *cheek pieces*, sewed at one end to 2 *square loops* 1·6 inches diameter, and the other to 2 *cheek rings* 1·6 inches diameter; 2 *standing loops* for the toggles of the watering bridle sewed to the cheek piece near to the square loops; 1 *crown piece* sewed to the *off* cheek ring, 1 buckle 1·12 inches, and *chape* sewed to the near cheek ring; 1 *nose band*, the ends sewed to the square loops; 1 *chin strap*, the ends sewed to the square loops and passing loose through the hitching-strap ring; 1 *throat strap*, folded on itself making two thicknesses, and forming at top a loop for the throat band to pass through, and embracing in the fold at the other end 1 *bolt* which holds 1 *hitching-strap ring*; 1 *throat band* passes loose through the loop in the throat strap, and is sewed to the cheek rings; 1 *hitching strap* 6½ feet long, 1 *buckle* 1·25 inches, and 1 *standing loop*, 1 *billet* sewed to the buckle end by the same seam which holds the buckle.

Saddle.

163. All the *leather* is black bridle or harness leather, and the buckles are blued malleable iron.

164. The *saddle* is composed of 1 *tree*, 2 *saddle skirts*, 2 *stirrups*, 1 *girth* and *girth strap*, 1 *surcingle*, 1 *crupper*.

Saddle Tree.

165. WOOD (beech)—1 *pommel* made of 2 pieces framed together at top and glued; 1 *cantle* formed of 2 pieces like the pommel; 2 *side bars* (poplar), each made of 3 pieces glued together; they are glued to the pommel and cantle, and fastened by 2 *rivets*, 2 *burrs*, and 4 *nails*, the burrs let in on the under side; 1 *strap mortise* in the pommel, 3 *strap mortises* in the cantle.

166. There are three sizes of trees, varying in the length of the seat. The number is marked on the pommel ornament.

No. 1.   11 inches length of seat.   15 per cent.
No. 2.   11½   "   "   50   "
No. 3.   12   "   "   35   "

167. IRON—1 *pommel arc* 0·1 inch thick, with three small holes on top, fastened to the side bars by 4 *rivets*; 1 *pommel plate* 0·1 inch thick, semicircular, fastened to the front of the pommel by 4 *rivets*; 1 *cantle arc* 0·1 inch thick, with three small holes on top, fastened to the side bars by 4 rivets; 1 *cantle plate* 0·1 inch thick, fastened to the rear of the cantle by 4 *rivets*; 2 *stirrup loops* hinged in 2 *holdfasts* which are fastened to the side bars by 6 *rivets*.

168. The tree is painted with one coat of white lead. It is covered with the best quality kip skin raw hide, put on wet, sewed with thongs of the same, and held in place by stitches through the wood along the junction of the pommel and cantle with the side bars. The seams are made on the edges of the side bars, where they will not chafe the horse or rider.

169. 2 *crupper rings*, held by staples driven into the front ends of side bars; 2 *foot staples* for coat straps, fastened to the front of the pommel by 4 *brass screws*, ¾ inch; 2 *crupper rings* (japanned black), fastened by staples driven into the rear ends of side bars; 2 *foot staples*, fastened to the rear of cantle by 4 brass screws, ¾ inch; 1 *guard plate*, 1 *pommel ornament* shield-shaped (sheet brass), fastened to the pommel, each, by 3 brass screw pins; 6 *guard plates*, fastened to the cantle by 12 *screw pins;* 2 *foot staples*, fastened on the back strap by 4 *brass screws*, ¾ inch; 1 *saddle-bag stud*, fastened on the back strap to the cantle arc by 2 copper rivets.

170. Two SADDLE SKIRTS (thick harness leather), fastened to the side bars by 38 brass screws, ¾ inch; 2 *stay loops* for the saddle-bag straps, sewed to the rear edge of the skirts.

171. Two STIRRUPS (hickory or oak), made of one piece bent, the ends separated by 1 *transom* and fastened by 2 *iron rivets*, each, 4 *burrs;* 2 *leather hoods*, fastened to the stirrups by 12 *copper rivets and burrs*—distance of hood from rear of stirrup, 6 inches; 2 *stirrup straps*, 2 *brass buckles*, 1·375 inches, 2 *sliding loops* pass through the stirrup loops and through a hole cut in the skirts; 2 *sweat leathers*, each has 2 *standing loops*.

172. GIRTH—2 *girth straps* pass over the pommel and cantle arcs, to which they are fastened by 4 *copper rivets* and 4 *burrs;* they are fastened to the side bars by 4 *brass screws*, ¾ inch; the ends are sewed into 2 D rings, 1·85 inches; 2 *girth billets*, sewed to the straight side of the D rings; 1 *girth*, 4·5 inches, blue woolen webbing; 1 *chape*, 1 *buckle*, 2 inches, 1 *standing loop*, and 1 *safe* on the off end; and 1 *chape*, 1 *buckle*, 1·5 inches, 1 D *ring*, 1·85 inches, 1 *standing loop*, 1 *safe* on the near side; 1 *standing loop* on the middle.

173. SIX COAT STRAPS, 6 *buckles*, 0·625 inch and stops. They pass through the mortises in the pommel and cantle and the foot staples.

174. ONE CARBINE SOCKET, 1 *strap*, 1 *buckle*, 0·75 inch, sewed to the socket. The socket is buckled on the D ring on the off side of the saddle.

175. ONE SURCINGLE, 3·25 inches, blue woolen webbing; 1 *chape*, 1 *buckle*, 1·5 inches, 1 *standing loop* on one end, and 1 *billet* on the other; 1 *billet* lining sewed over the end of webbing to the billet; 2 *standing loops* near the buckle end.

176. CRUPPER—1 *dock*, made of a single piece and stuffed with hair, the ends sewed to the body of the crupper; 1 *body*, split at one end, has sewed to it 1 *chape*, 1 *ring*, 1·25 inches, 2 *back straps*—each has one buckle, 0·75 inch, and 2 *sliding loops*—they pass through the rings of the side bars and the ring on the body of the crupper.

177. SADDLE BAGS (bag leather).—They are composed of 2 *pouches* and 1 *seat;* the ends of the seat are sewed to the pouches. Each pouch has 1 *back*, sewed to the gusset and upper part of inner front with a *welt;* 1 *gusset*, sewed to the back and to 1 *outer* and 1 *inner front* with a *welt;* 1 *flap*, sewed to the top of the back and to the seat by 2 seams; 1 *flap billet*, sewed to the point of the flap; 1 *chape and* 1 *buckle*, 0·625 inch, sewed to the outer front; 1 *billet*, 1 *buckle*, 0·625 inch, sewed to the chape. The seat is sewed to the pouch by the same seams which join the flap to the back of the pouch. It has 2

holes for the foot staples and 1 *hole* for the saddle-bag stud; 2 *key straps*, sewed to the seat near its ends; 4 *lacing thongs* for the pouches.

178. SADDLE BLANKET.—To be of pure wool, close woven, of stout yarns of an indigo-blue color, with an orange border 3 inches wide, 3 inches from the edge. The letters U. S., 6 inches high, of orange color, in the centre of the blanket. Dimensions: 75 inches long, 67 inches wide; weight, 3·1875 pounds; variation allowed in weight, 0·1875 pounds.

179. SPURS (brass)—2 *spurs*, 2 *rowels*, 2 *rivets*, 2 *spur straps*, 19 inches long, 2 *roller buckles*, 0·625 inch, 2 *standing loops*.

Length of heel for No. 1, 3½ inches; for No. 2, 3¼ inches—inside measure.

Width of heel   "   3¼   "   "   3   "   "

Length of shank to centre of rowel, 1 inch.

Diameter of rowel, 0·85 inch.

180. ONE HORSE BRUSH—1 *body* (maple), Russia bristles; 1 *cover*, glued and fastened to the body by 8 brass screws; 1 *hand strap*, fair leather, fastened to the sides of the body by 6 screws; 2 *leather washers* under the heads of screws. *Dimensions:* Body, 9·25 inches long, 4 inches wide, 0·5 inch thick; cover, 0·1 inch thick; bristles project 0·9 inch; hand strap, 2 inches wide.

181. ONE CURRY-COMB—iron, japanned black. The pattern of "Carpenter's, No. 333." 1 *body* (sheet-iron, 0·4), the top and bottom edges turned at right angles, forming two rows of teeth; 3 *double rows* of teeth, riveted to the body by *six rivets;* 1 *cross bar*, riveted across the top by 2 rivets; 1 *handle shank*, riveted to the body by 3 rivets; 1 *handle* (wood), turned and painted, passes over the shank and is held by the riveted end of the shank; 1 *ferrule*, sheet-iron. *Dimensions:* Length, 4 inches; width, 4·75 inches; thickness, 0·75 inch; length of handle, 4 inches; weight, 0·84 pound.

182. ONE PICKET PIN (iron, painted black)—The parts are: *the body, the neck, the head, the swell, the point;* 1 *lariat ring* around the neck, 8-shaped, the larger opening for the lariat. *Dimensions:* Length, 14 inches; diameter at swell, 4 inches from point, 0·75 inch; at neck, 0·5 inch; at head, 1 inch; lariat ring, 0·2 inch wire, welded, interior diameter, 1 inch; weight of pin, 1·29 pounds.

183. ONE LARIAT—Best hemp 1¼-inch rope, 30 feet long, of 4 strands; an eye spliced in one end, the other end whipped with small twine; weight, 2·38 pounds.

184. ONE LINK—1 *strap*, embracing in the fold at one end 1 *spring hook*, and at the other 1 *buckle*, 0·75 inch, and 1 *billet*.

185. ONE NOSE BAG—same as for Light Artillery.

MILITARY STORE-KEEPERS.

186. A citizen's frock-coat of blue cloth, with buttons of the department to which they are attached; round black hat; pantaloons and vest, plain, white or dark blue; cravat or stock, black.

MISCELLANEOUS.

187. General Officers, and Colonels having the brevet rank of General Officers, may, on occasions of ceremony, and when not serving with troops, wear the "dress" and "undress" prescribed by existing regulations.

188. Officers below the grade of Colonel having brevet rank, will wear the epaulettes and shoulder-straps distinctive of their army rank. In all other respects, their uniform and dress will be that of their respective regiments, corps, or departments, and according to their commission in the same. Officers above the grade of Lieutenant-Colonel by ordinary commission, having brevet rank, may wear the uniform of their respective regiments or corps, or that of General Officers, according to their brevet rank.

189. The uniform and dress of the Signal Officer will be that of a Major of the General Staff.

190. Officers are permitted to wear a plain dark blue body-coat, with the button designating their respective corps, regiments, or departments, without any other mark or ornament upon it. Such a coat, however, is not to be considered as a dress for any military purpose.

191. In like manner, officers are permitted to wear a buff, white, or blue vest, with the small button of their corps, regiment, or department.

192. Officers serving with mounted troops are allowed to wear, for stable duty, a plain dark blue cloth jacket, with one or two rows of buttons down the front, according to rank ; stand-up collar, sloped in front as that of the uniform coat ; shoulder-straps according to rank, but no other ornament.

193. The hair to be short ; the beard to be worn at the pleasure of the individual ; but, when worn, to be kept short and neatly trimmed.

194. *A Band* will wear the uniform of the regiment or corps to which it belongs. The commanding officer may, at the expense of the corps, sanctioned by the Council of Administration, make such *additions* in ornaments as he may judge proper.

Flags, Colors, Standards, Guidons.

GARRISON FLAG.

195. The garrison flag is the national flag. It is made of bunting, thirty-six feet fly, and twenty feet hoist, in thirteen horizontal stripes of equal breadth, alternately red and white, beginning with the red. In the upper quarter, next the staff, is the union, composed of a number of white stars, equal to the number of States, on a blue field, one-third the length of the flag, extending to the lower edge of the fourth red stripe from the top. The storm flag is twenty feet by ten feet ; the recruiting flag, nine feet nine inches by four feet four inches.

COLORS OF ARTILLERY REGIMENTS.

196. Each regiment of Artillery shall have two silken colors. The first, or the national color, of stars and stripes, as described for the garrison flag. The number and name of the regiment to be embroidered with gold on the centre stripe. The second, or regimental color, to be yellow, of the same dimensions as the first, bearing in the centre two cannon crossing, with the letters U. S. above, and the number of the regiment below ; fringe, yellow. Each color to be six feet six inches fly, and six feet deep

on the pike. The pike, including the spear and ferrule, to be nine feet ten inches in length. Cords and tassels, red and yellow silk intermixed.

COLORS OF INFANTRY REGIMENTS.

197. Each regiment of Infantry shall have two silken colors. The first, or the national color, of stars and stripes, as described for the garrison flag; the number and name of the regiment to be embroidered with silver on the centre stripe. The second or regimental color, to be blue, with the arms of the United States embroidered in silk on the centre. The name of the regiment in a scroll, underneath the eagle. The size of each color to be six feet six inches fly, and six feet deep on the pike. The length of the pike, including the spear and ferrule, to be nine feet ten inches. The fringe yellow; cords and tassels blue and white silk intermixed.

CAMP COLORS.

198. The camp colors are of bunting, eighteen inches square; white for infantry, and red for artillery, with the number of the regiment on them. The pole eight feet long.

STANDARDS AND GUIDONS OF MOUNTED REGIMENTS.

199. Each regiment will have a silken standard, and each company a silken guidon. The standard to bear the arms of the United States, embroidered in silk, on a blue ground, with the number and name of the regiment, in a scroll underneath the eagle. The flag of the standard to be two feet five inches wide, and two feet three inches on the lance, and to be edged with yellow silk fringe.

200. The flag of the guidon is swallow-tailed, three feet five inches from the lance to the end of the swallow-tail; fifteen inches to the fork of the swallow-tail, and two feet three inches on the lance. To be half red and half white, dividing at the fork, the red above. On the red, the letters U. S. in white; and on the white, the letter of the company in red. The lance of the standards and guidons to be nine feet long, including spear and ferrule.

Table of Pay, Subsistence, etc.,

ALLOWED BY LAW TO THE OFFICERS OF THE ARMY.

RANK AND CLASSIFICATION OF OFFICERS.	PAY.	SUBSISTENCE.		SERVANTS.			FORAGE FURNISHED FOR HORSES.	
	Per Month.	Number of Rations per day.	Monthly Commutation Value.	Number of Servants allowed.	Monthly Commutation Value.	Total Monthly Pay.	In time of War.	In time of Peace.
General Officers.								
Lieutenant-General, ...	$270 00	40	$360 00	4	$90 00	$720 00		$50
Aides-de-camp and Military Secretary to Lieutenant-General, *each*, ...	80 00	5	45 00	2	45 00	170 00		2
Major-General, ...	220 00	15	135 00	4	90 00	445 00		5
Senior Aide-de-camp to General-in-Chief, . .	80 00	4	36 00	2	47 00	163 00		2
Aide-de-camp, in addition to pay, &c., of Lieutenant or Captain, ...	24 00	...	....	...	....	24 00		2
Brigadier-General, ...	124 00	12	108 00	3	67 50	209 50		4
Aide-de-camp, in addition to pay, &c., of Lieutenant, ...	20 00	...	....	...	....	11*		2
Adjutant-General's Department.								
Adjutant-General—Brigadier-General, . . .	124 00	24	216 00	3	67 50	407 50		4
Assistant Adjutant-General—Colonel, . . .	110 00	6	54 00	2	47 00	211 00		2
Assistant Adjutant-General—Lieut.-Col., . .	95 00	5	45 00	2	47 00	187 00		2
Assistant Adjutant-General—Major, ...	80 00	4	36 00	2	47 00	163 00		2
Judge-Advocate-General—Colonel, ...	110 00	6	54 00	2	47 00	211 00		2
Judge-Advocate—Major, ...	80 00	4	36 00	2	47 00	163 00		2
" " (Division)—Major, . . .	80 00	4	36 00	2	47 00	163 00		2
Inspector-General's Department.								
Inspector-General—Colonel, ...	110 00	6	54 00	2	47 00	211 00		2
Assistant Inspector-General—Major, . . .	80 00	4	36 00	2	47 00	163 00		2
Signal Department.								
Signal Officer—Colonel, ...	110 00	6	54 00	2	47 00	211 00		2
Quartermaster's Department.								
Quartermaster-General—Brigadier-General, .	124 00	24	216 00	3	67 00	407 50		4
Assistant Quartermaster-General—Colonel, .	110 00	6	54 00	2	47 00	211 00		2

TABLE OF PAY, SUBSISTENCE, FORAGE.—Continued.

RANK AND CLASSIFICATION OF OFFICERS.	PAY.	SUBSISTENCE.		SERVANTS.			FORAGE FURNISHED FOR HORSES.	
	Per Month.	Number of Rations per day.	Monthly Commutation Value.	Number of Servants allowed.	Monthly Commutation Value.	Total Monthly Pay.	In time of War.	In time of Peace.
Quartermaster's Department.								
Deputy Quartermaster-General—Lt.-Col., . .	$95 00	5	$45 00	2	$47 00	$187 00		$2
Quartermaster—Major, ...	80 00	4	36 00	2	47 00	163 00		2
Assistant Quartermaster—Captain, ...	70 00	4	36 00	1	23 50	129 50		2
Subsistence Department.								
Commissary-General of Subs.—Brig.-Gen., .	124 00	12	108 00	3	67 00	299 00		4
Assistant Commissary-General of Subsistence— Lieutenant-Colonel, ...	95 00	5	45 00	2	47 00	187 00		2
Commissary of Subsistence—Major, . . .	80 00	4	36 00	2	47 00	163 00		2
Commissary of Subsistence—Captain, . . .	70 00	4	36 00	1	23 50	129 50		2
Assistant Commissary of Subsistence, in addition to pay, &c., of Lieutenant, . . .	20 00	...	....	...	....	11*		...
Medical Department.								
Surgeon-General—Brigadier-General, ...	124 00	12	108 00	3	67 50	299 50		4
Assistant Surgeon-General, ...	110 00	6	54 00	2	47 00	211 00		2
Medical Inspector-General, ...	110 00	6	54 00	2	47 00	211 00		2
Medical Inspectors, ...	95 00	5	45 00	2	47 00	187 00		2
Surgeons of ten years' service, ...	80 00	8	72 00	2	47 00	199 00		2
Surgeons of less than ten years' service, . .	80 00	4	36 00	2	47 00	163 00		2
Assistant Surgeons of ten years' service, . .	70 00	8	72 00	1	23 50	165 50		2
Assistant Surgeons of five years' service, . .	70 00	4	36 00	1	23 50	129 50		2
Assistant Surgeons of less than five years' service, . .	53 33	4	36 00	1	23 50	112 83		2
Pay Department.								
Paymaster-General, $2,740 per annum, . . .	....	...	....	...	....	288 33		...
Deputy Paymaster-General, ...	95 00	5	45 00	2	47 00	187 00		2
Paymaster, ...	80 00	4	36 00	2	47 00	163 00		2
Officers of the Corps of Engineers, Corps of Topographical Engineers, and Ordnance Department.								
Chief of Ordnance—Brigadier-General, . . .	124 00	24	216 00	3	67 50	407 50		4
Colonel, ...	110 00	6	54 00	2	47 00	211 00		2
Lieutenant-Colonel, ...	95 00	5	45 00	2	47 00	187 00		2
Major, ...	80 00	4	36 00	2	47 00	163 00		2
Captain, ...	70 00	4	36 00	1	23 50	129 50		2
First Lieutenant, ...	53 33	4	36 00	1	23 50	112 83		2
Second Lieutenant, ...	53 33	4	36 00	1	23 50	112 83		2
Brevet Second Lieutenant, ...	53 33	4	36 00	1	23 50	112 83		2
Officers of Mounted Dragoons, Cavalry, Riflemen, and Light Artillery.								
Colonel, ...	110 00	6	54 00	2	47 00	211 00		2
Lieutenant-Colonel, ...	95 00	5	45 00	2	47 00	187 00		2

TABLE OF PAY, SUBSISTENCE, FORAGE.—Continued.

RANK AND CLASSIFICATION OF OFFICERS.	PAY.	SUBSISTENCE.		SERVANTS.			FORAGE FURNISHED FOR HORSES.	
	Per Month.	Number of Rations per day.	Monthly Commutation Value.	Number of Servants allowed.	Monthly Commutation Value.	Total Monthly Pay.	In time of War	In time of Peace.
Officers of Mounted Dragoons, Cavalry, Riflemen, and Light Artillery.								
Major, ...	$80 00	4	$36 00	2	$47 00	$163 00		$2
Captain, ...	70 00	4	36 00	1	23 50	129 50		2
First Lieutenant, ...	53 33	4	36 00	1	23 50	112 83		2
Second Lieutenant, ...	53 33	4	36 00	1	23 50	112 83		2
Brevet Second Lieutenant, ...	53 33	4	36 00	1	23 50	112 83		2
Adjutant, Regimental Quartermaster, { in addition to pay of Lieutenant, } Regimental Commissary,	10 00	...	....	...	....	10 00		...
Officers of Artillery and Infantry.								
Colonel, ...	95 00	6	54 00	2	45 00	194 00		2
Lieutenant-Colonel, ...	80 00	5	45 00	2	45 00	170 00		2
Major, ...	70 00	4	36 00	2	45 00	151 00		2
Captain, ...	60 00	4	36 00	1	22 50	118 50		...
First Lieutenant, ...	50 00	4	36 00	1	22 50	108 50		...
Second Lieutenant, ...	45 00	4	36 00	1	22 50	103 50		...
Brevet Second Lieutenant, ...	45 00	4	36 00	1	22 50	103 50		...
Adjutant, in addition to pay, &c., of Lieutenant,	10 00	...	....	...	....	10 00		2
Regimental Quartermaster, in addition to pay, &c., of Lieutenant, ...	10 00					10 00		2
Military Storekeepers.								
Attached to the Quartermaster's Department; at armories, and at arsenals of construction; the storekeeper at Watertown Arsenal, and storekeepers of ordnance serving in Oregon, California, and New Mexico, $1,490 per annum, ...	....	...	....	...	....	....		...
At all other arsenals, $1,040 per annum, . . .	....	...	....	...	....	....		...
Chaplains, ...	100 00	2	18 00	...	....	118 00		1

Paymaster's clerks, $700 per annum, and one ration (75 cents) per day when on duty.

The officer in command of a company is allowed $10 per month for the responsibility of clothing, arms, and accoutrements.—Act 2 March, 1827, Sec. 2.

* Subaltern officers, employed on the *General Staff*, and receiving increased pay therefor, are not entitled to the additional or fourth ration provided by the Act of 2 March, 1827, Sec. 2.

Every commissioned officer below the rank of Brigadier-General receives one additional ration per day for every five years' service.—Act 5 July, 1836, Sec. 12, and 7 July, 1838, Sec. 9.

Forage is commuted only when the Government cannot furnish it in kind, and then at $8 per month for each horse actually kept by the officer.

MONTHLY PAY OF NON-COMMISSIONED OFFICERS, PRIVATES, ETC.

CAVALRY.

Sergeant-Major,	$21 00	Hospital Steward,	$30 00
Quartermaster-Sergeant,	21 00	Corporal,	14 00
Chief Bugler or Trumpeter,	21 00	Bugler or Trumpeter,	13 00
First Sergeant,	20 00	Farrier and Blacksmith,	15 00
Sergeant,	17 00	Private,	13 00
Saddler Sergeant,	21 00	Veterinary Surgeon,	75 00
Commissary Sergeant,	21 00	African Under Cooks,	10 00

ORDNANCE.

Sergeant,	$34 00	Saddler,	$14 00
Corporal,	20 00	Private, first class,	17 00
Wagoner,	14 00	Private, second class,	13 00

ARTILLERY AND INFANTRY.

Sergeant-Major,	$21 00	Corporal,	$13 00
Quartermaster-Sergeant,	21 00	Artificer, artillery,	15 00
Commissary-Sergeant,	21 00	Private,	13 00
First Sergeant,	20 00	Principal Musician,	21 00
Sergeant,	17 00	Musician,	12 00
Hospital Stewards,	30 00	African Under Cooks,	10 00

SAPPERS, MINERS, AND PONTONIERS.

Sergeant,	$34 00	Private, second class,	$13 00
Corporal,	20 00	Musician,	12 00
Private, first class,	17 00	African Under Cooks,	10 00

BRIGADE BANDS.

Leader,	$45 00	Eight of the Band,	$17 00
Four of the Band,	34 00	Four of the Band,	20 00
Medical Cadets,	$30 00	Matron,	$6 00
Hospital Steward, first class,	22 00	Female Nurses, 40 cents per day and one ration.	
" " second class,	20 00		

Two dollars per month is to be retained from the pay of each private soldier until the expiration of his term of enlistment, and 12½ cents per month from all enlisted men, for the support of the "Soldiers' Home."

All enlisted men are entitled to $2 per month additional pay for re-enlisting, and $1 per month for each subsequent period of five years' service, provided they re-enlist within one month after the expiration of their term.

Volunteers and militia, when called into service of the United States, are entitled to the same pay, allowances, &c., as regulars.

Medical Storekeepers, same as Military Storekeepers, Quartermaster's Department.

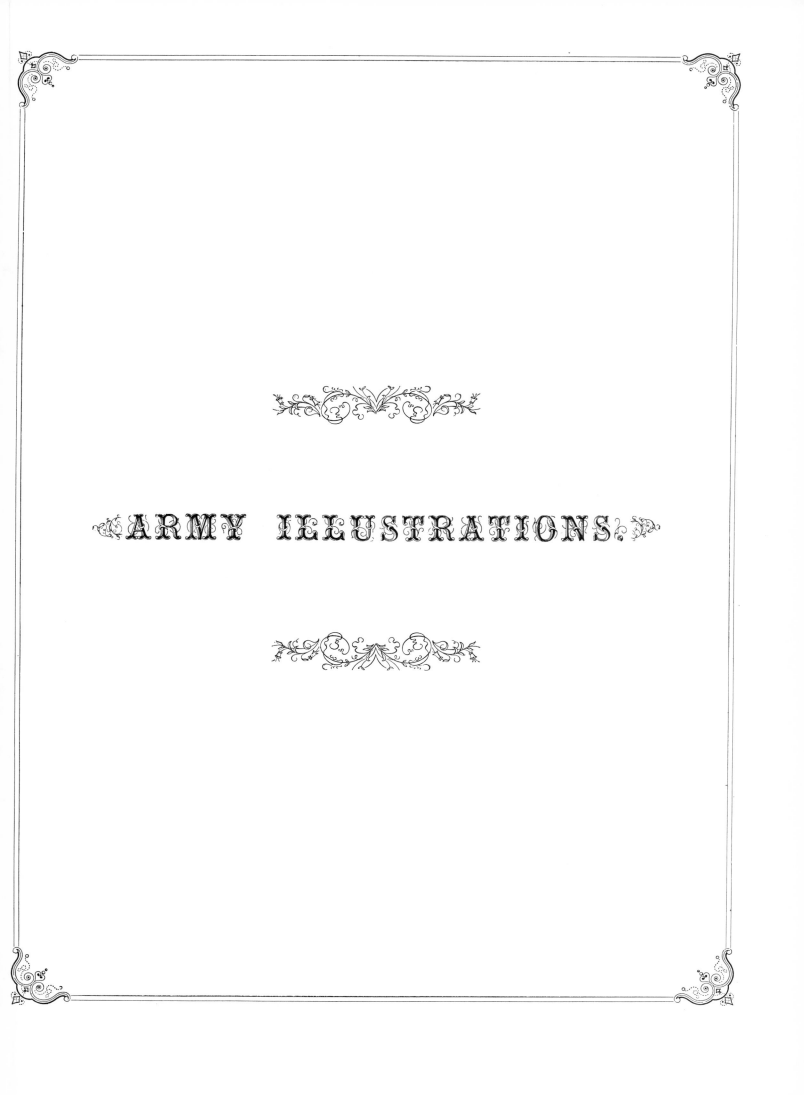

ARMY ILLUSTRATIONS.

Rich Presentation Swords—Solid Silver Scabbard.

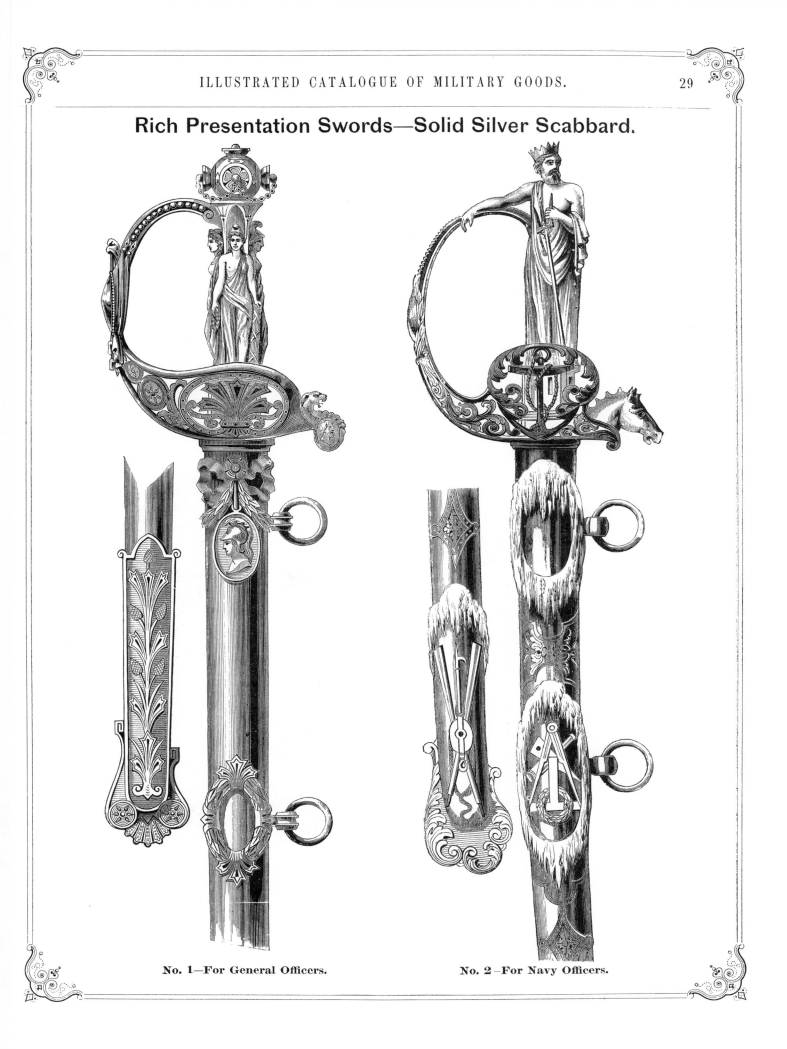

No. 1—For General Officers.   No. 2—For Navy Officers.

Rich Presentation Swords.

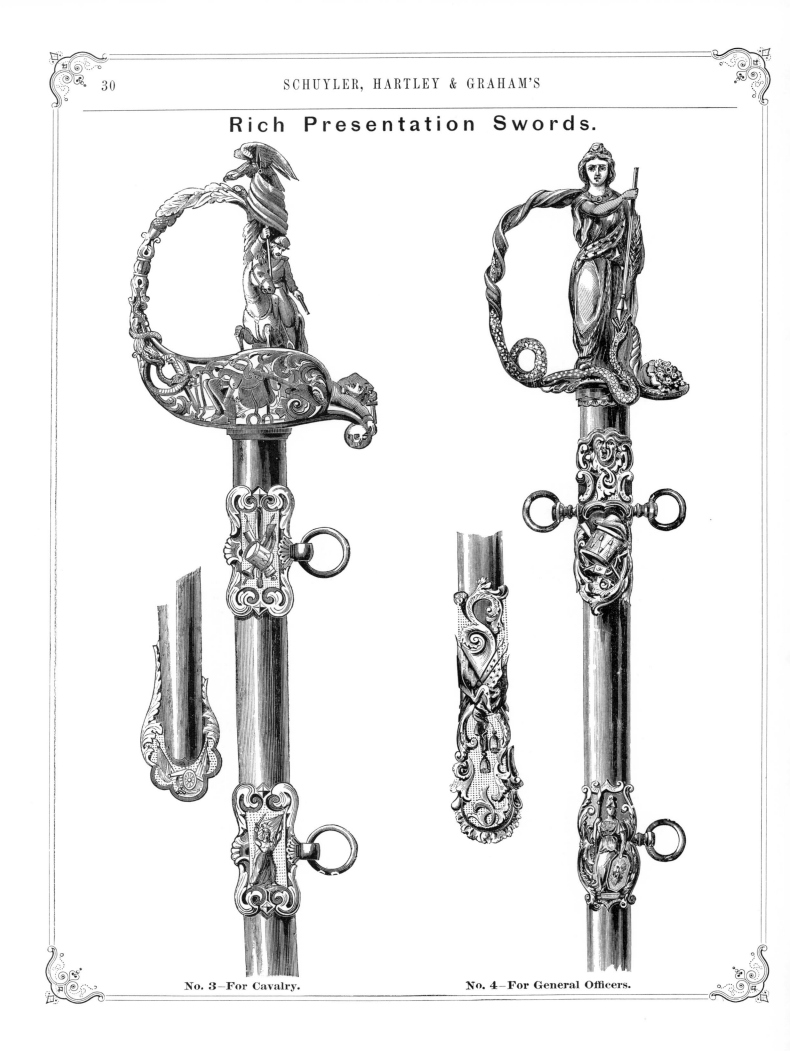

No. 3—For Cavalry.   No. 4—For General Officers.

Rich Presentation Swords for General Officers.
SOLID SILVER SCABBARD.

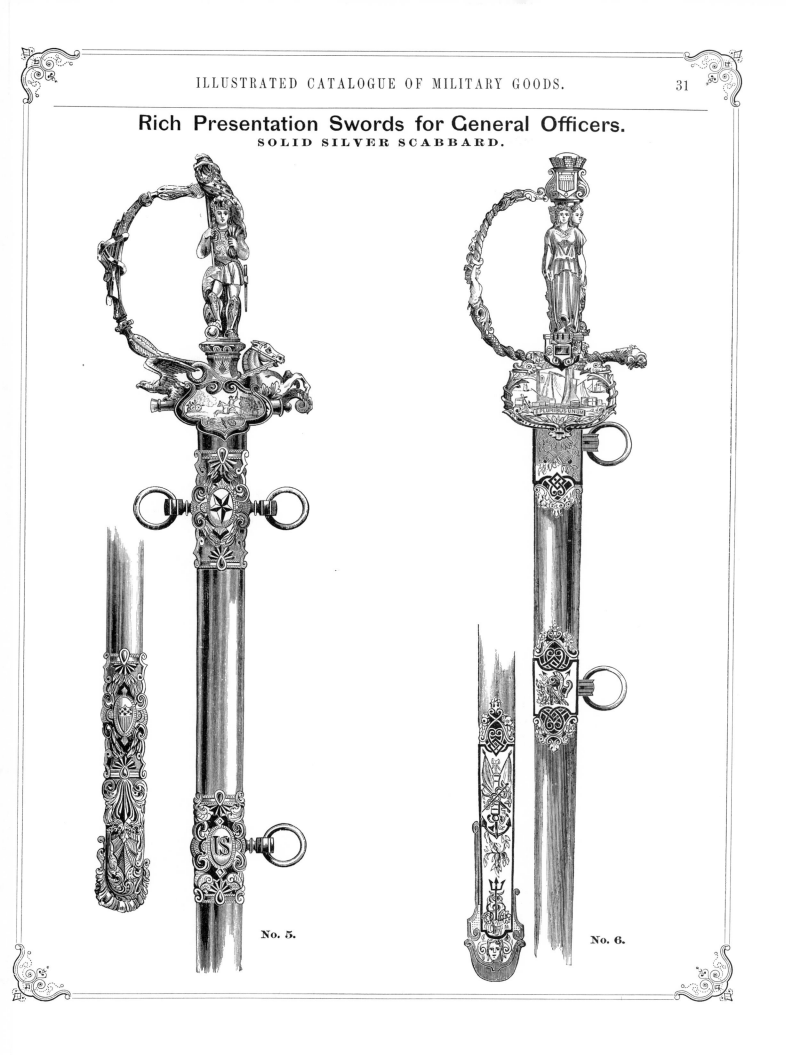

No. 5.

No. 6.

Rich Presentation Swords for General Officers.
SOLID SILVER SCABBARD.

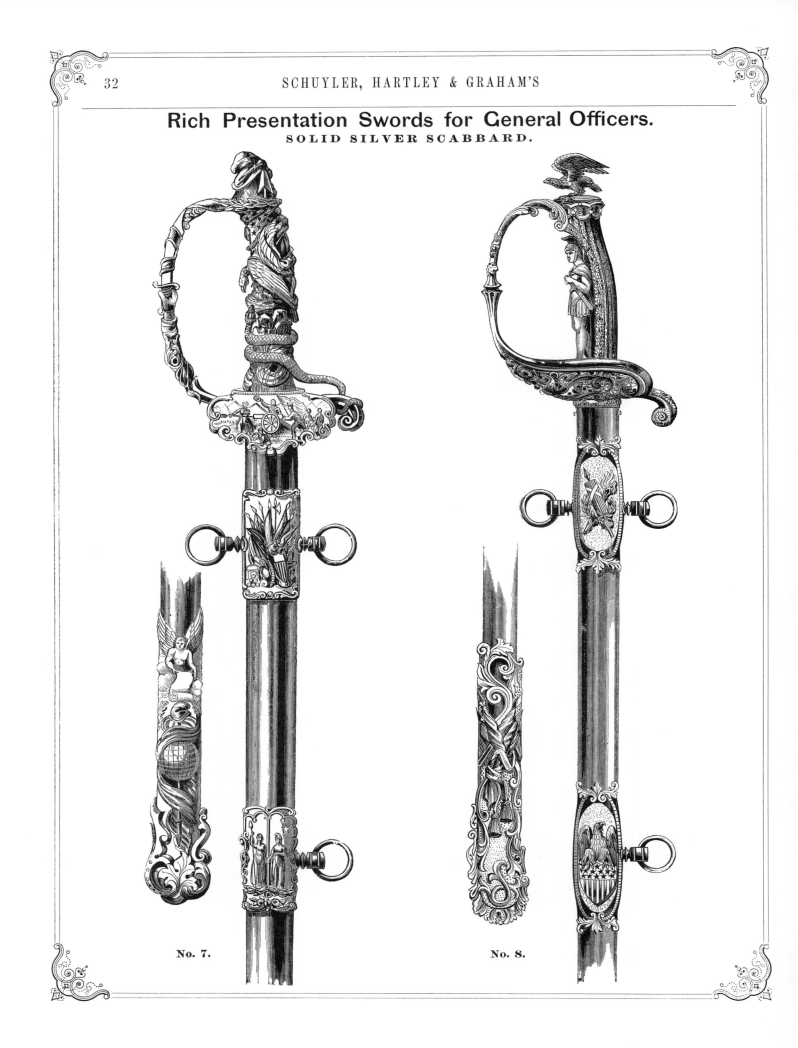

No. 7.   No. 8.

Rich Presentation Swords for Field & Line Officers.

No. 9.

No. 10.

Rich Presentation Swords for Field & Line Officers.

No. 11.

No 12.

Rich Presentation Swords for Field & Line Officers.

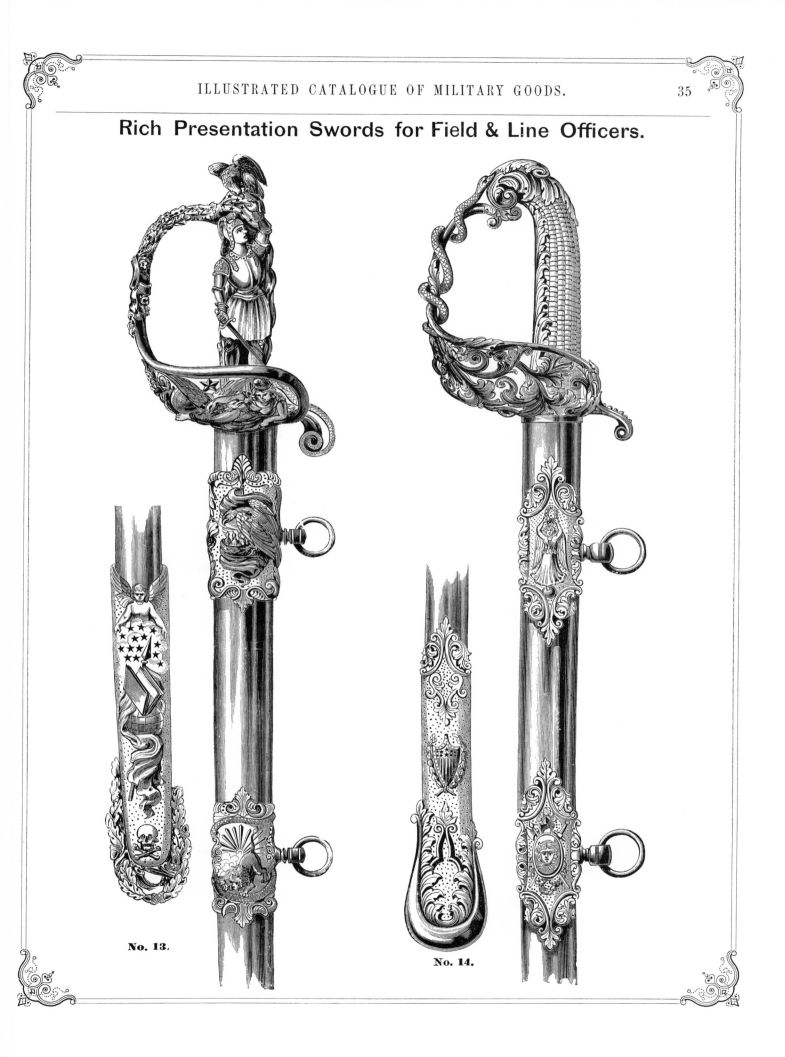

No. 13.　　　No. 14.

Rich Presentation Swords for Field & Line Officers.

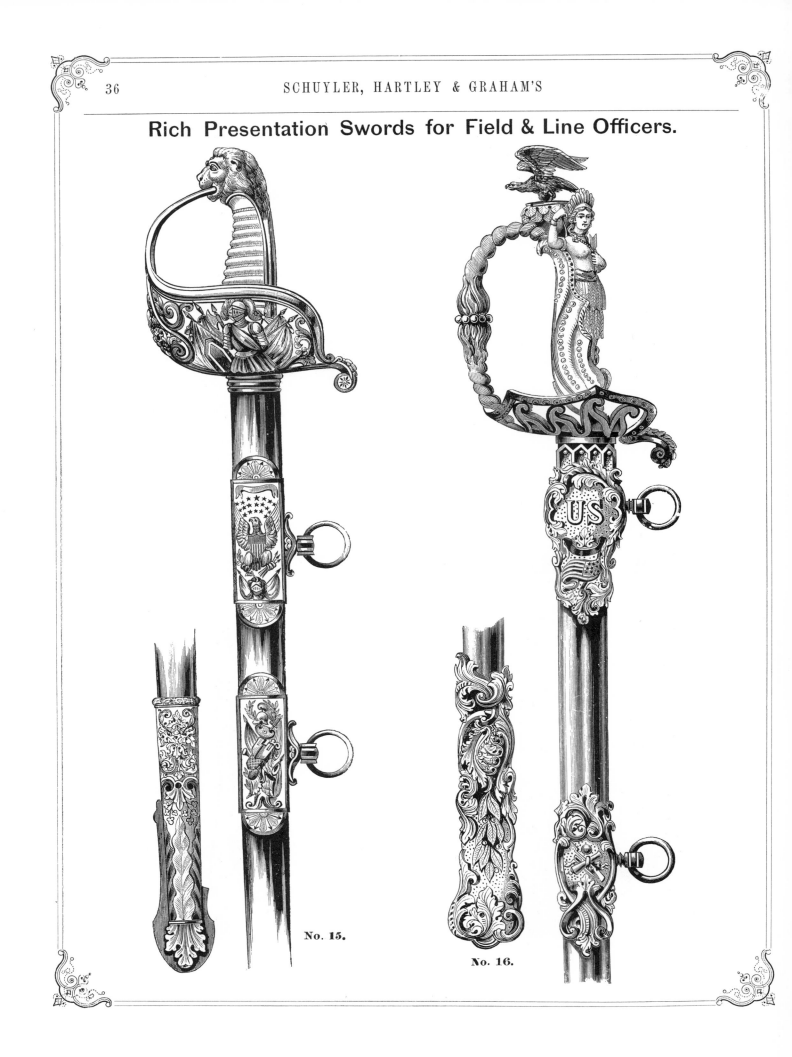

No. 15.

No. 16.

Rich Presentation Sabres for Cavalry Officers.

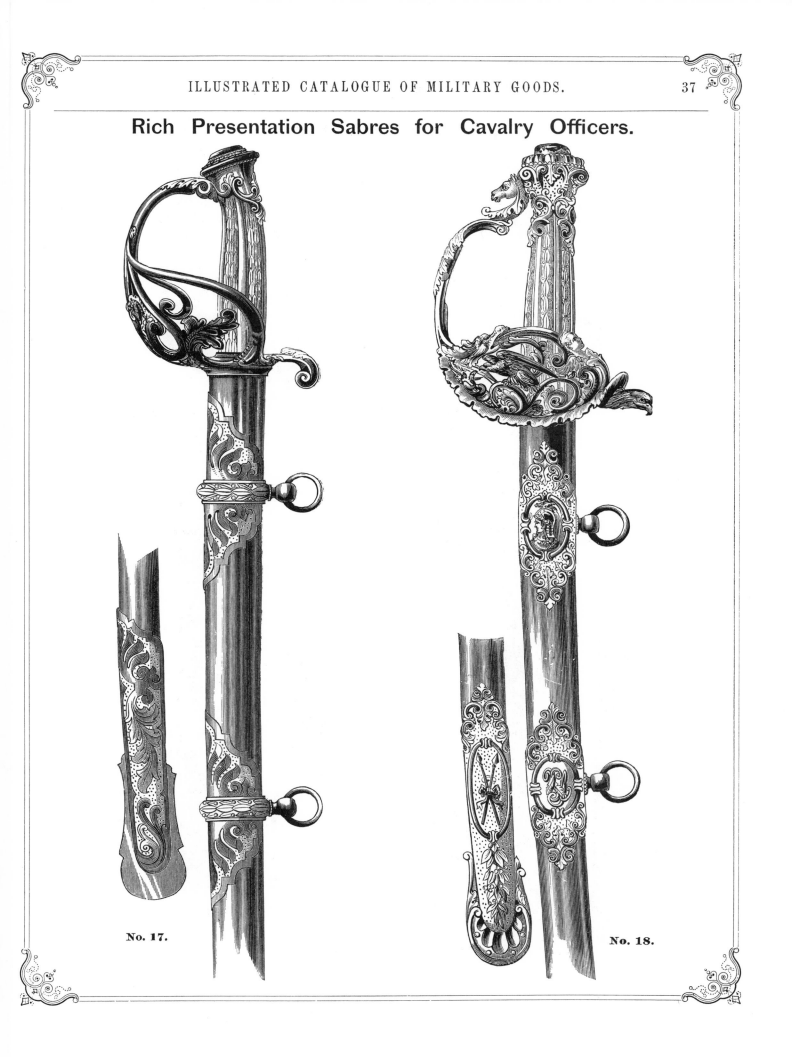

No. 17.

No. 18.

Rich Presentation Sabres for Cavalry Officers.

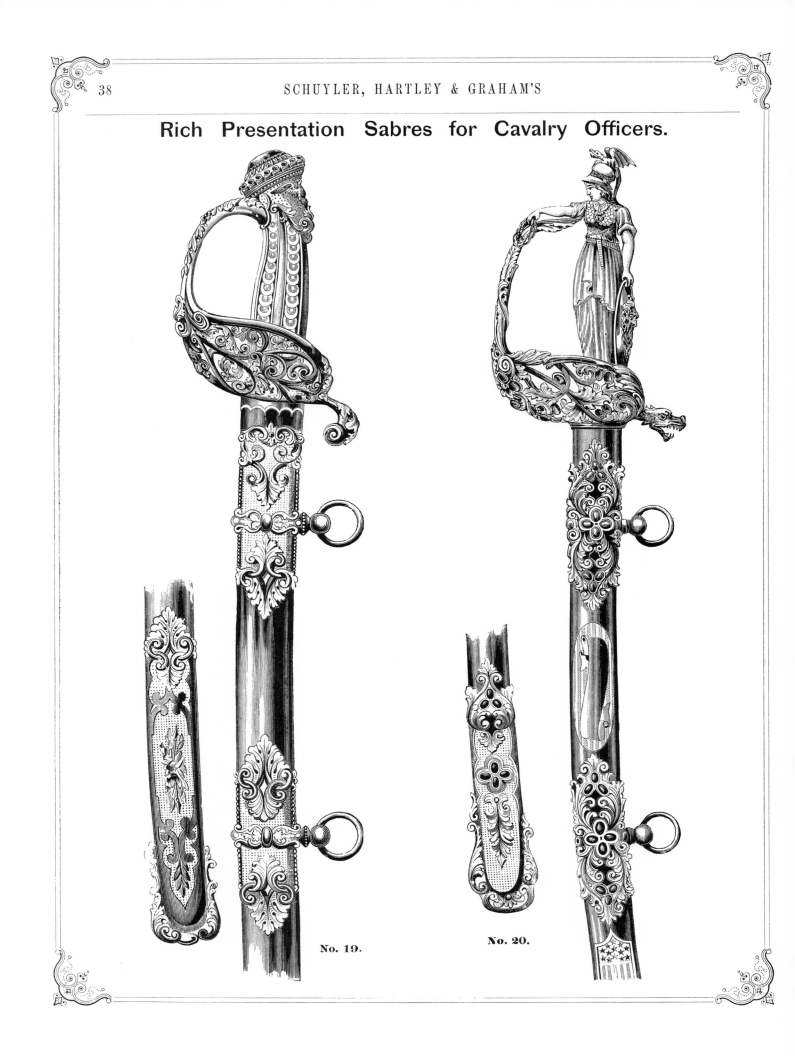

No. 19.   No. 20.

U. S. Regulation Swords.

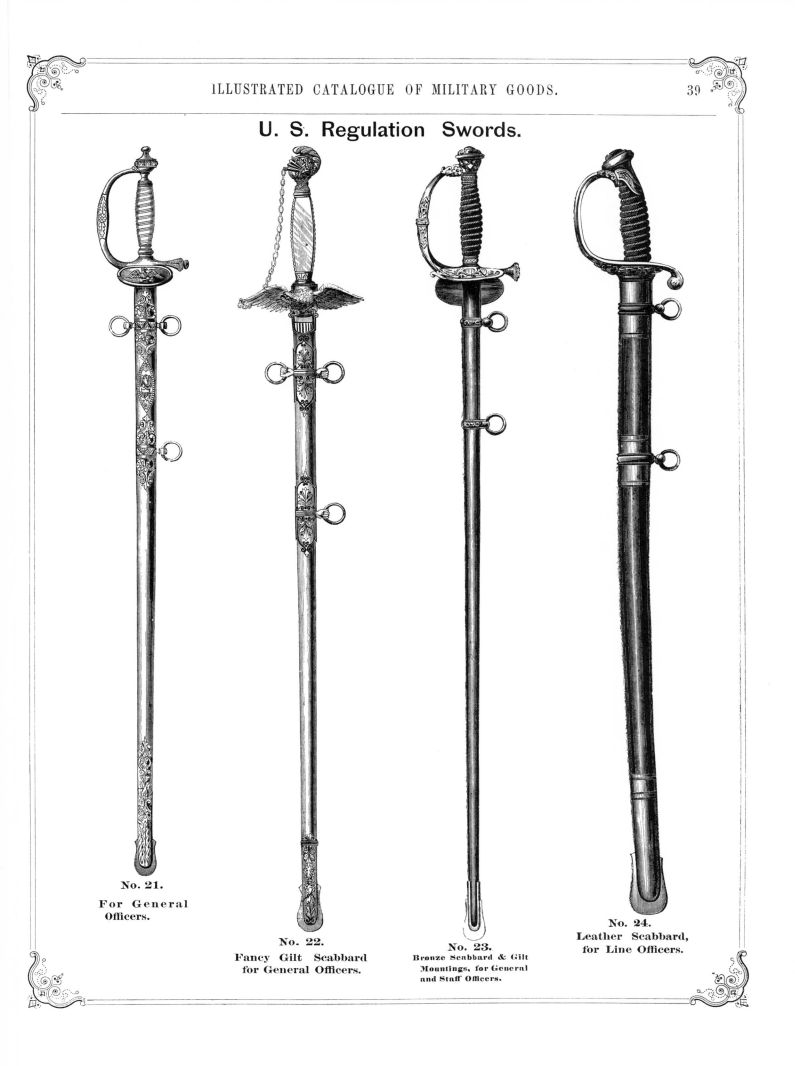

No. 21.
For General
Officers.

No. 22.
Fancy Gilt Scabbard
for General Officers.

No. 23.
Bronze Scabbard & Gilt
Mountings, for General
and Staff Officers.

No. 24.
Leather Scabbard,
for Line Officers.

U. S. Regulation Swords.

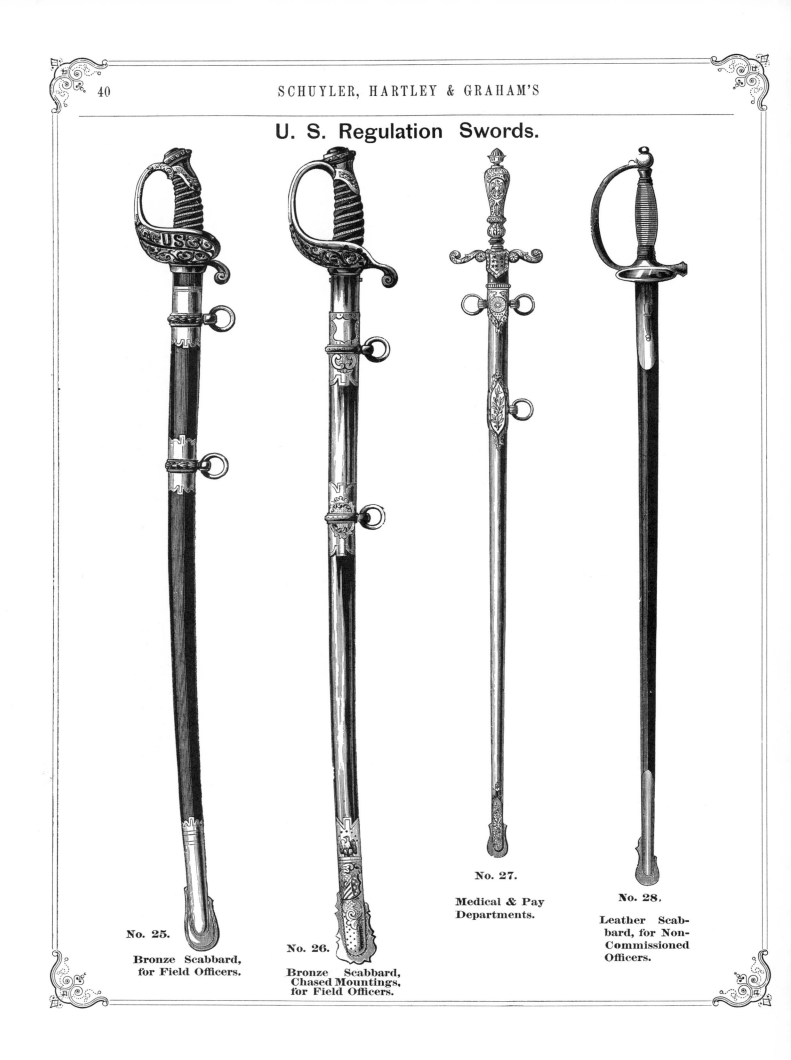

No. 25.

**Bronze Scabbard,
for Field Officers.**

No. 26.

**Bronze Scabbard,
Chased Mountings,
for Field Officers.**

No. 27.

**Medical & Pay
Departments.**

No. 28.

**Leather Scab-
bard, for Non-
Commissioned
Officers.**

Steel Scabbard Swords.

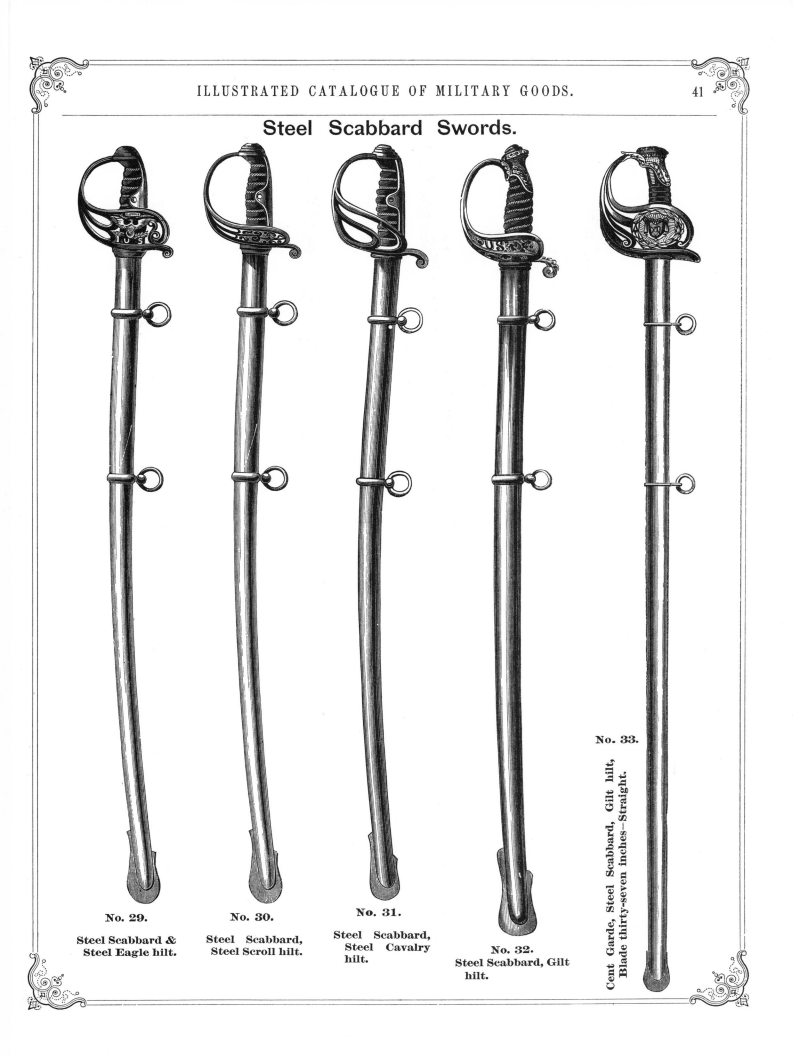

No. 29.

**Steel Scabbard &
Steel Eagle hilt.**

No. 30.

**Steel Scabbard,
Steel Scroll hilt.**

No. 31.

**Steel Scabbard,
Steel Cavalry
hilt.**

No. 32.

**Steel Scabbard, Gilt
hilt.**

No. 33.

**Cent Garde, Steel Scabbard, Gilt hilt,
Blade thirty-seven inches—Straight.**

Sabres and Masonic Swords.

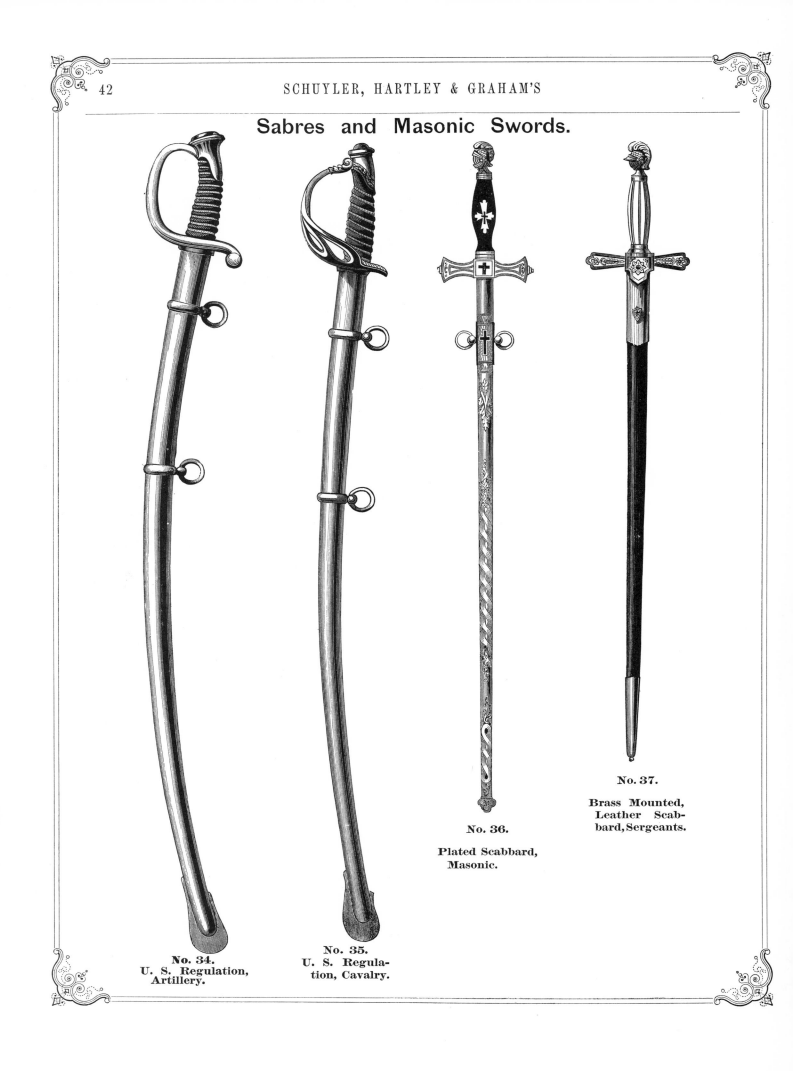

No. 34.
U. S. Regulation,
Artillery.

No. 35.
U. S. Regula-
tion, Cavalry.

No. 36.

Plated Scabbard,
Masonic.

No. 37.

Brass Mounted,
Leather Scab-
bard, Sergeants.

Sword Knots.

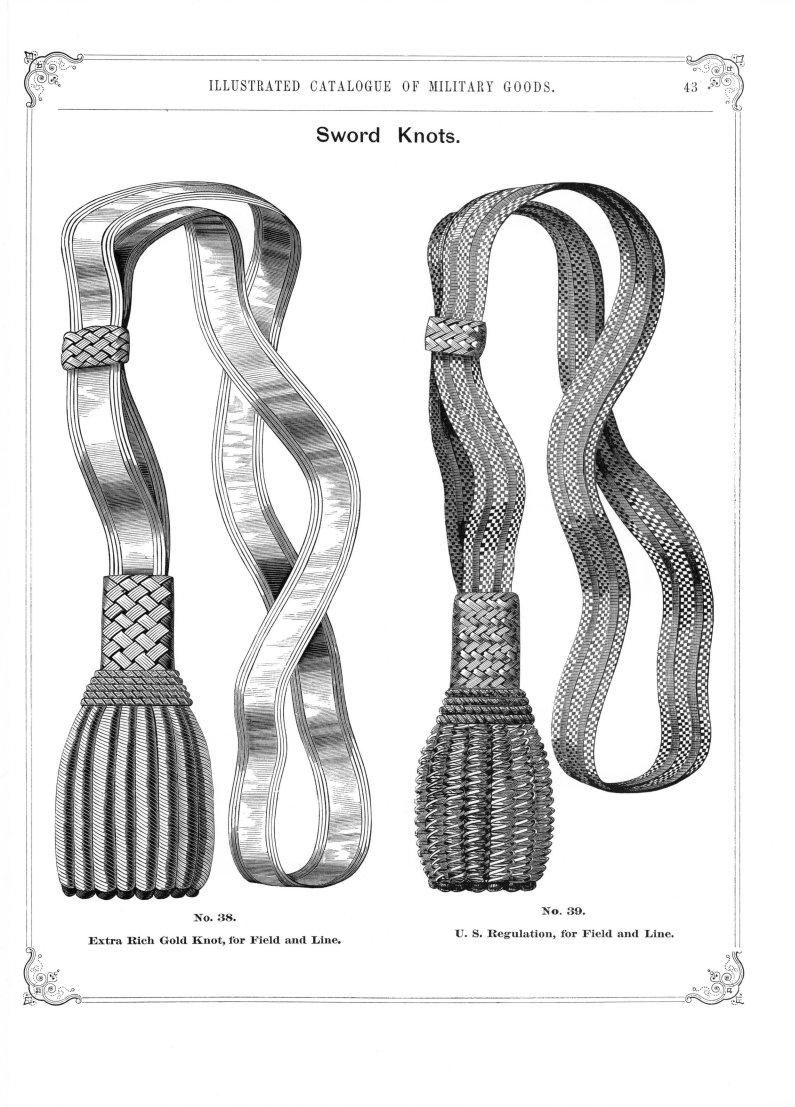

No. 38.

Extra Rich Gold Knot, for Field and Line.

No. 39.

U. S. Regulation, for Field and Line.

Sword Knots.

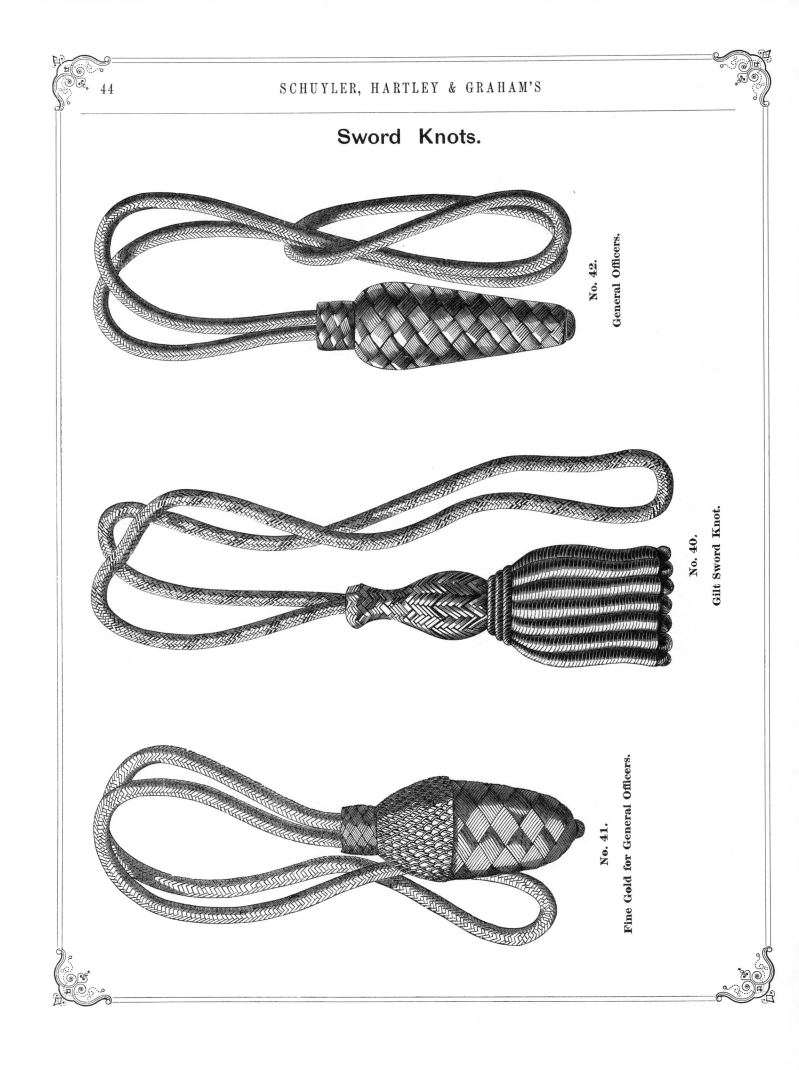

No. 42.
General Officers.

No. 40.
Gilt Sword Knot.

No. 41.
Fine Gold for General Officers.

Sword Belts.

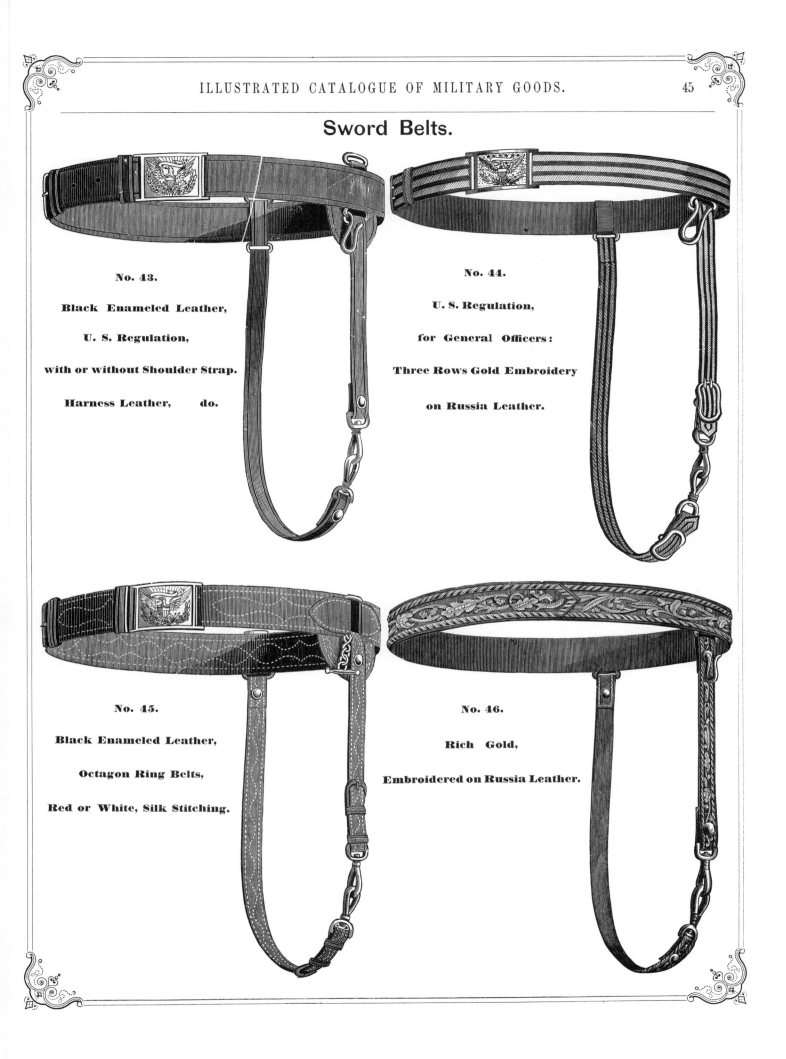

No. 43.

Black Enameled Leather,

U. S. Regulation,

with or without Shoulder Strap.

Harness Leather,   do.

No. 44.

U. S. Regulation,

for General Officers:

Three Rows Gold Embroidery

on Russia Leather.

No. 45.

Black Enameled Leather,

Octagon Ring Belts,

Red or White, Silk Stitching.

No. 46.

Rich Gold,

Embroidered on Russia Leather.

Embroidered Sword Belts for Presentation.

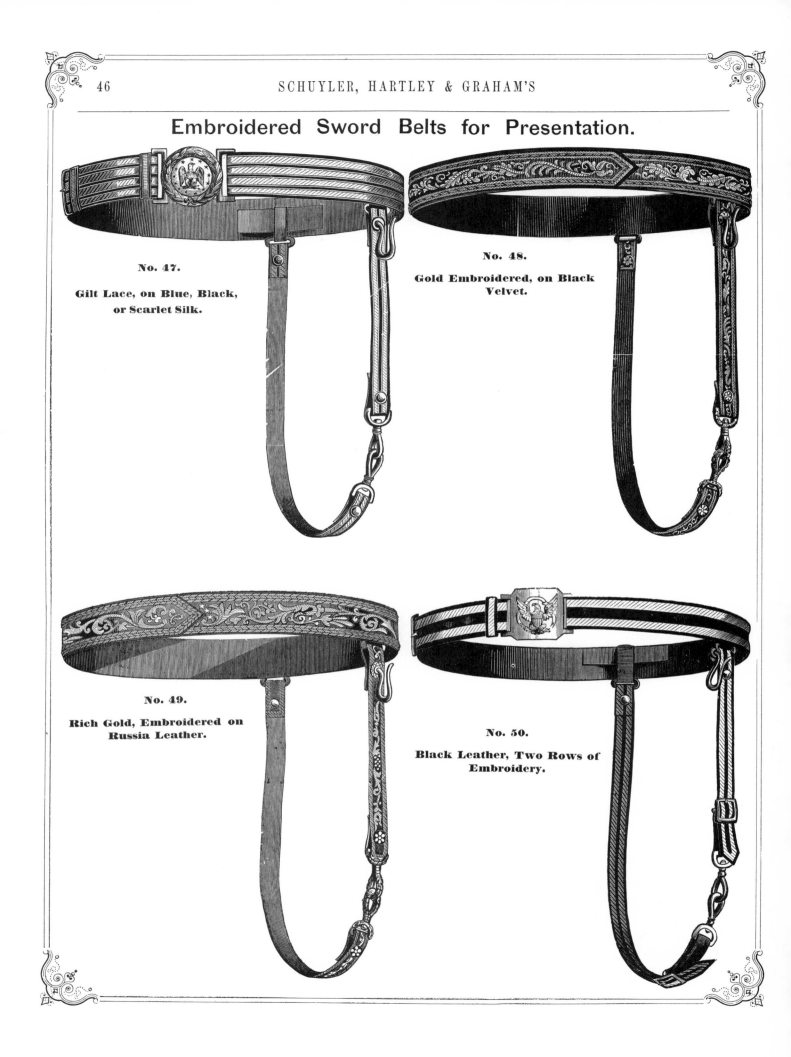

No. 47.

Gilt Lace, on Blue, Black, or Scarlet Silk.

No. 48.

Gold Embroidered, on Black Velvet.

No. 49.

Rich Gold, Embroidered on Russia Leather.

No. 50.

Black Leather, Two Rows of Embroidery.

Gauntlets, Belt Plates, &c.

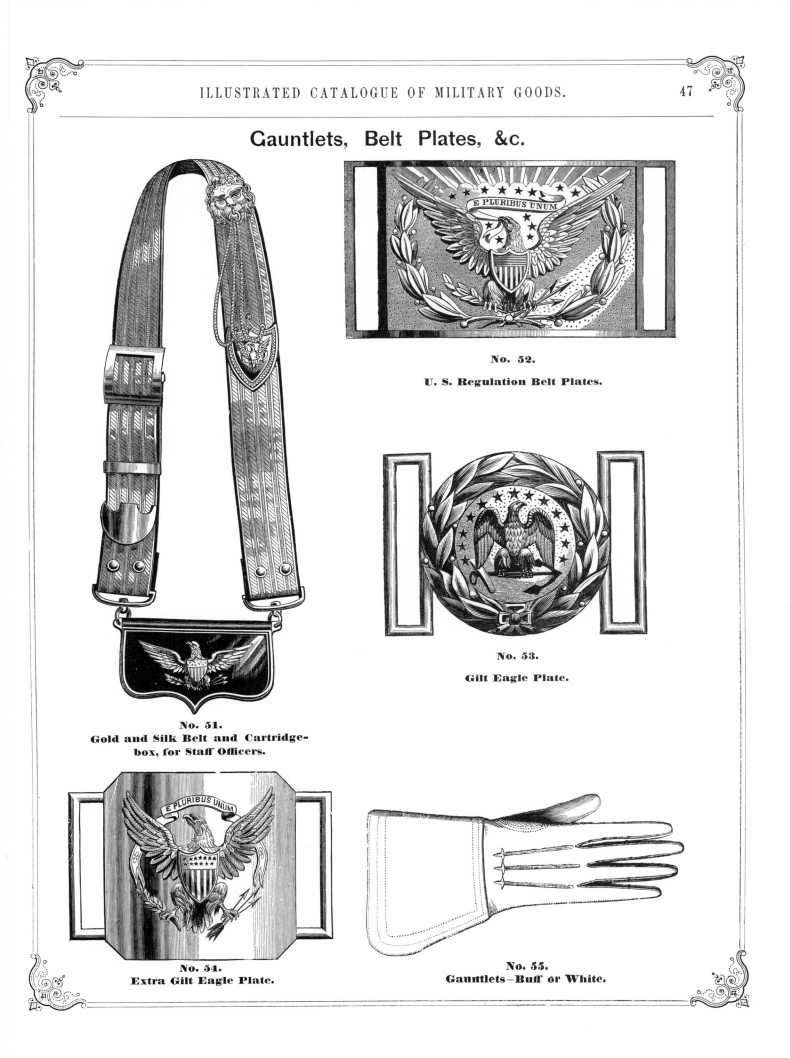

No. 52.

U. S. Regulation Belt Plates.

No. 53.

Gilt Eagle Plate.

No. 51.

Gold and Silk Belt and Cartridge-box, for Staff Officers.

No. 54.

Extra Gilt Eagle Plate.

No. 55.

Gauntlets—Buff or White.

Chapeaux, Hats, and Caps.

No. 56.

U. S. A. Regulation Chapeau.

No. 57.

U. S. Felt Hat.

No. 58.

Fatigue Cap, with Oiled Silk Cover.

No. 59.

Fatigue Cap, with Gold, or Silk Braid.

No. 60.

Burnside Pattern Felt Hat.

No. 60½.

Artillery Cap.

No. 61.

Plated Metal Figures, for Officers' Caps.

No. 62.

Company Letters, Brass or Plated.
Company Figures, do.　do.

Hat Cords.

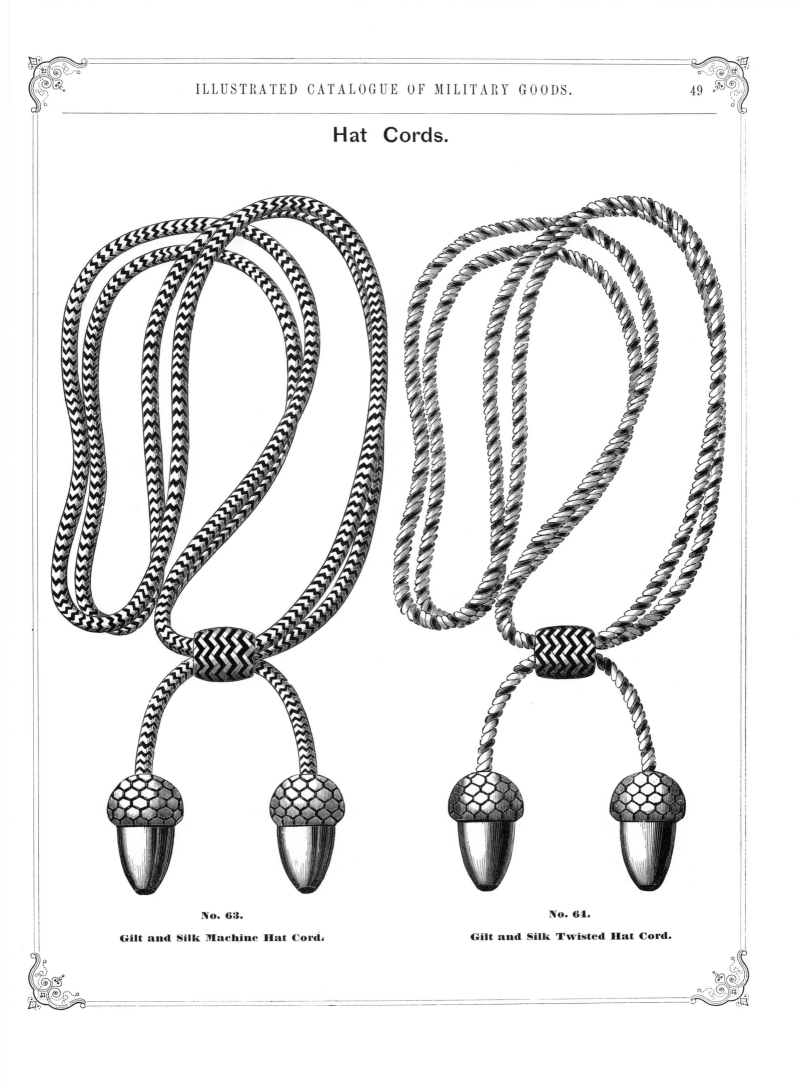

No. 63.

Gilt and Silk Machine Hat Cord.

No. 64.

Gilt and Silk Twisted Hat Cord.

Hat Cord, Coat Sling, Knapsack, &c.

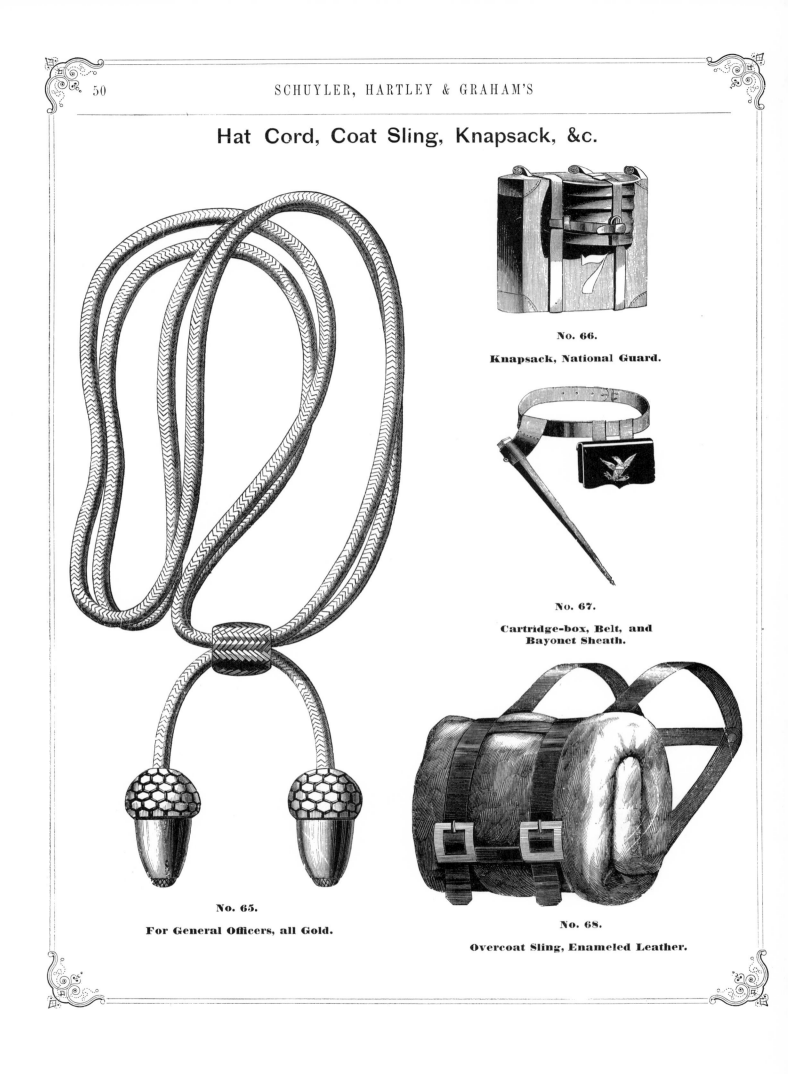

No. 66.

Knapsack, National Guard.

No. 67.

Cartridge-box, Belt, and Bayonet Sheath.

No. 65.

For General Officers, all Gold.

No. 68.

Overcoat Sling, Enameled Leather.

Russian, or Artillery Shoulder Knots.

No. 70.

Gold Knots, without ornaments, for Major.
do.   do.   Silver Emb'd Leaf, for Lt.-Col.
do.   do.   do.   do. Eagle, for Colonel.

No. 69.

Gold Knots, Three Rows, without ornament, for 2d Lieutenant.
do.   do.   with One Silver Emb'd Bar, for 1st Lieutenant.
do.   do.   with Two do.   do.   Bars, for Captain.

No. 71.

Gold Knots, Fancy Cord.

Ornaments within Crescents of Epaulettes.

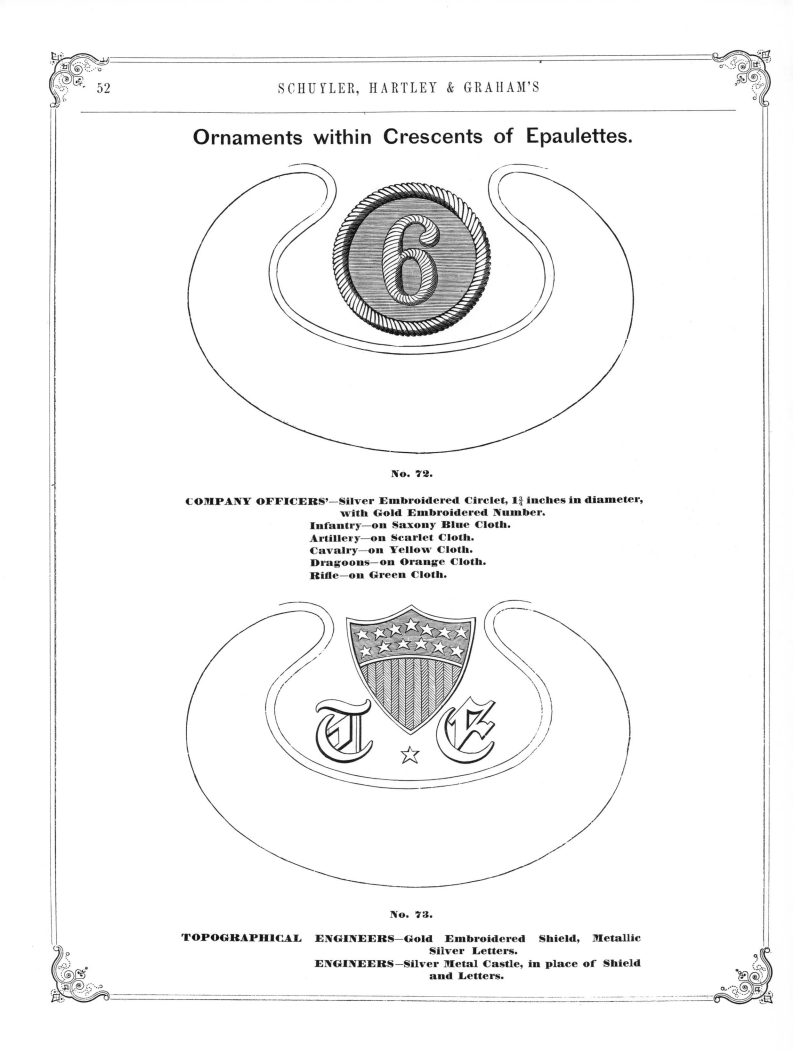

No. 72.

COMPANY OFFICERS'—Silver Embroidered Circlet, 1¾ inches in diameter, with Gold Embroidered Number.
Infantry—on Saxony Blue Cloth.
Artillery—on Scarlet Cloth.
Cavalry—on Yellow Cloth.
Dragoons—on Orange Cloth.
Rifle—on Green Cloth.

No. 73.

TOPOGRAPHICAL ENGINEERS—Gold Embroidered Shield, Metallic Silver Letters.
ENGINEERS—Silver Metal Castle, in place of Shield and Letters.

Ornaments within Crescents of Epaulettes.

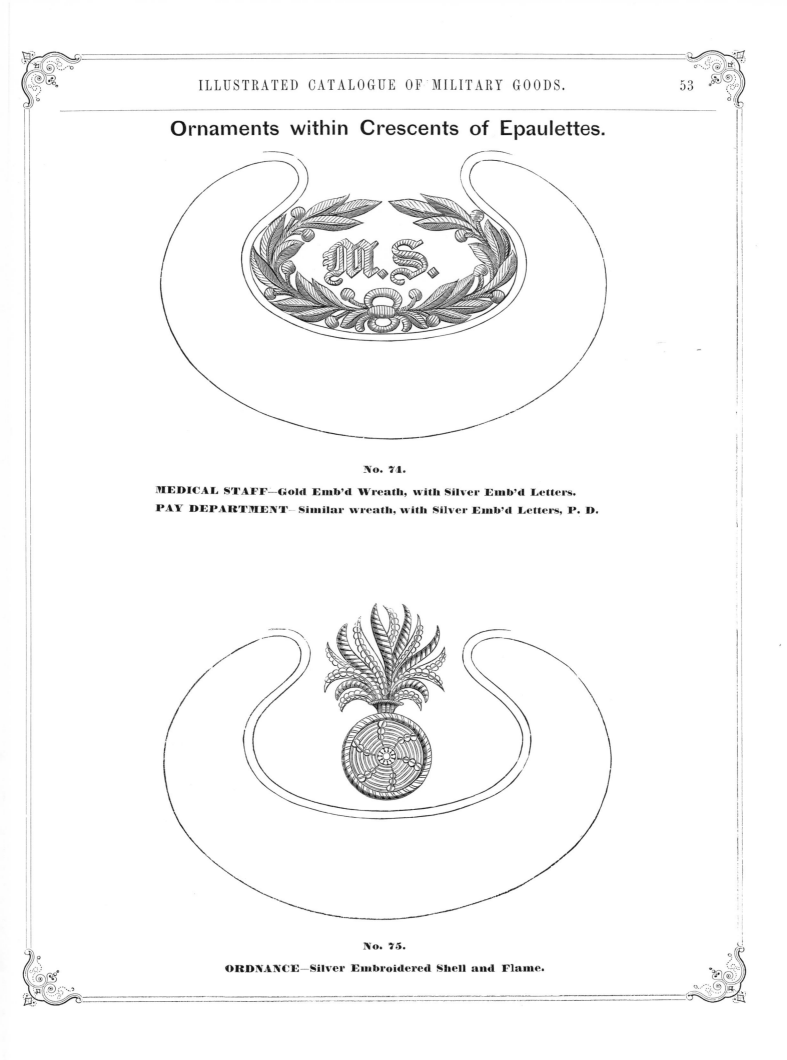

No. 74.

MEDICAL STAFF—Gold Emb'd Wreath, with Silver Emb'd Letters.
PAY DEPARTMENT— Similar wreath, with Silver Emb'd Letters, P. D.

No. 75.

ORDNANCE—Silver Embroidered Shell and Flame.

Ornaments on Strap of Epaulettes, designating Rank.

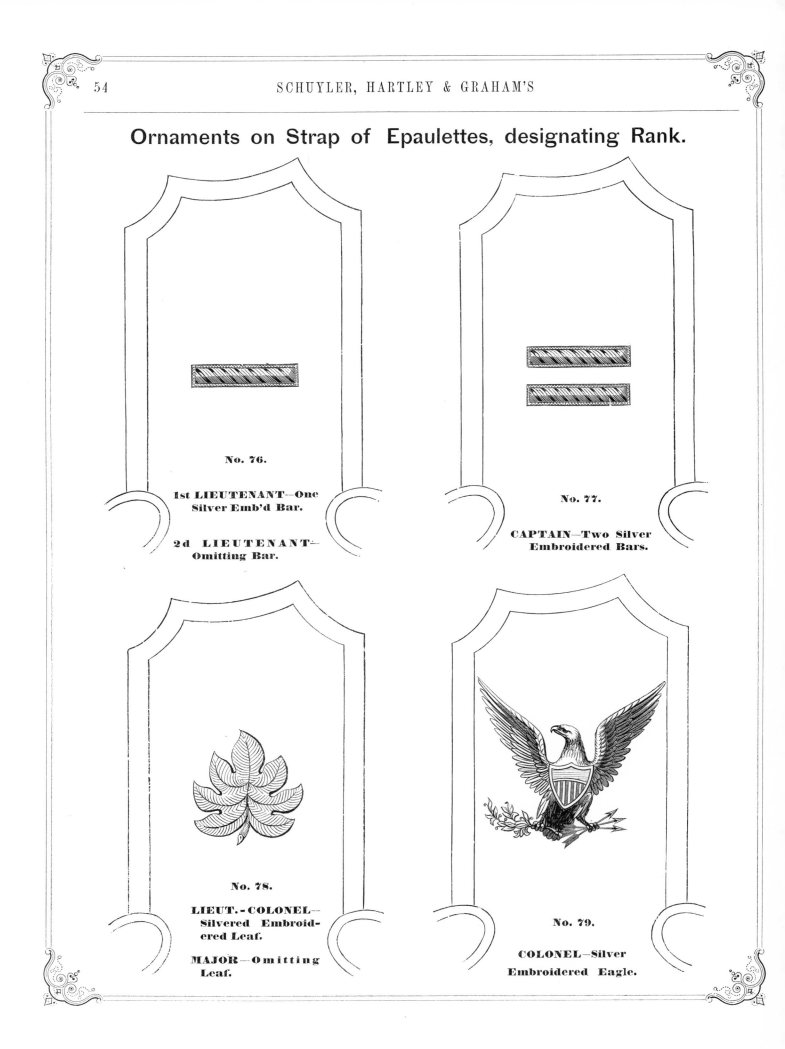

No. 76.

1st LIEUTENANT—One Silver Emb'd Bar.

2d LIEUTENANT—Omitting Bar.

No. 77.

CAPTAIN—Two Silver Embroidered Bars.

No. 78.

LIEUT.-COLONEL—Silvered Embroidered Leaf.

MAJOR—Omitting Leaf.

No. 79.

COLONEL—Silver Embroidered Eagle.

Ornaments on Strap of Epaulettes, designating Rank.

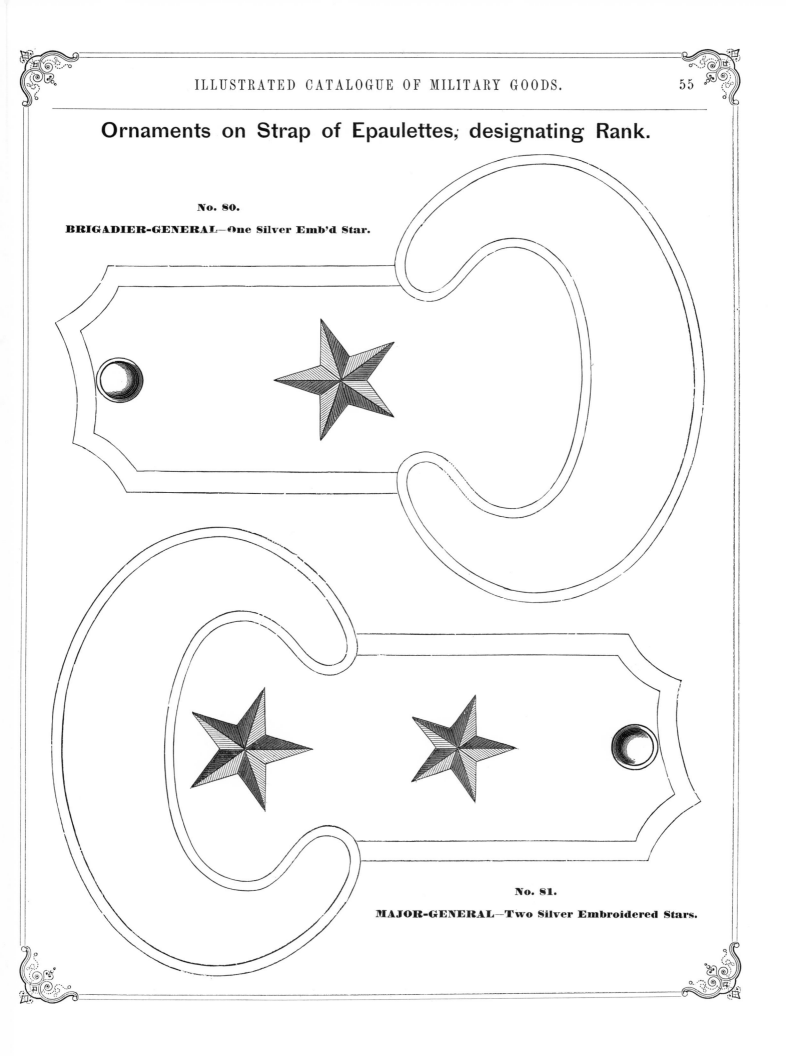

No. 80.

BRIGADIER-GENERAL—One Silver Emb'd Star.

No. 81.

MAJOR-GENERAL—Two Silver Embroidered Stars.

Epaulettes for General—dead and bright bullion.

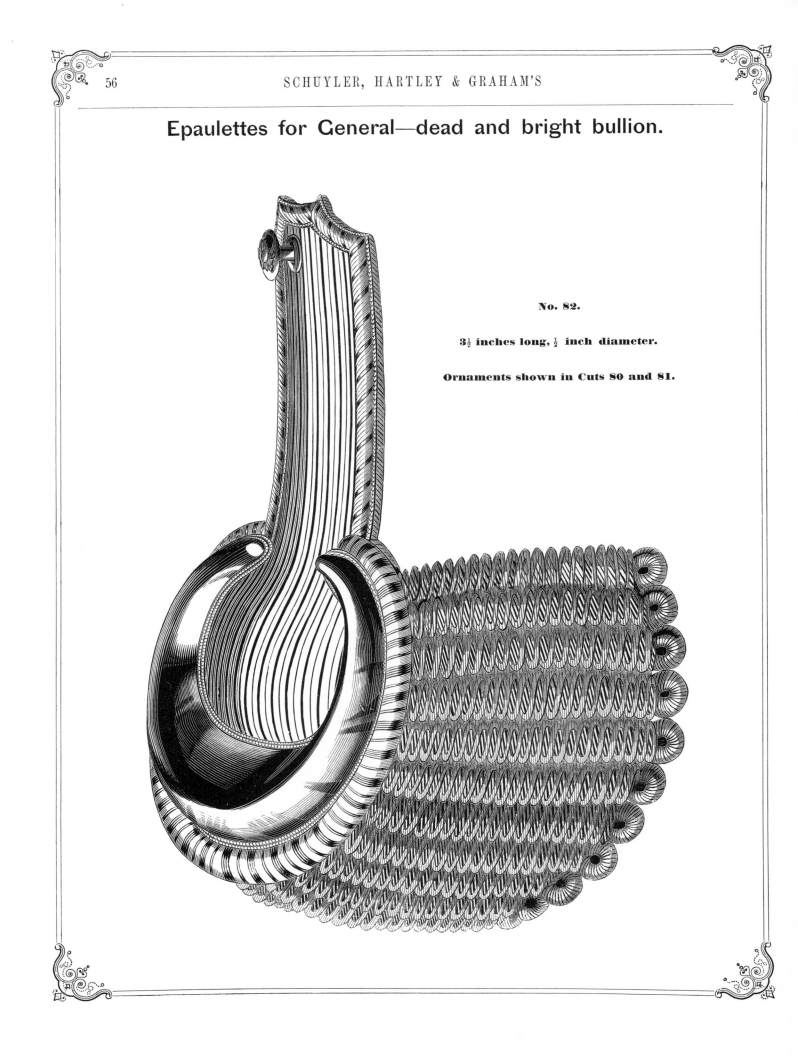

No. 82.

3½ inches long, ½ inch diameter.

Ornaments shown in Cuts 80 and 81.

Epaulettes for Colonel, Lieutenant-Colonel, and Major.

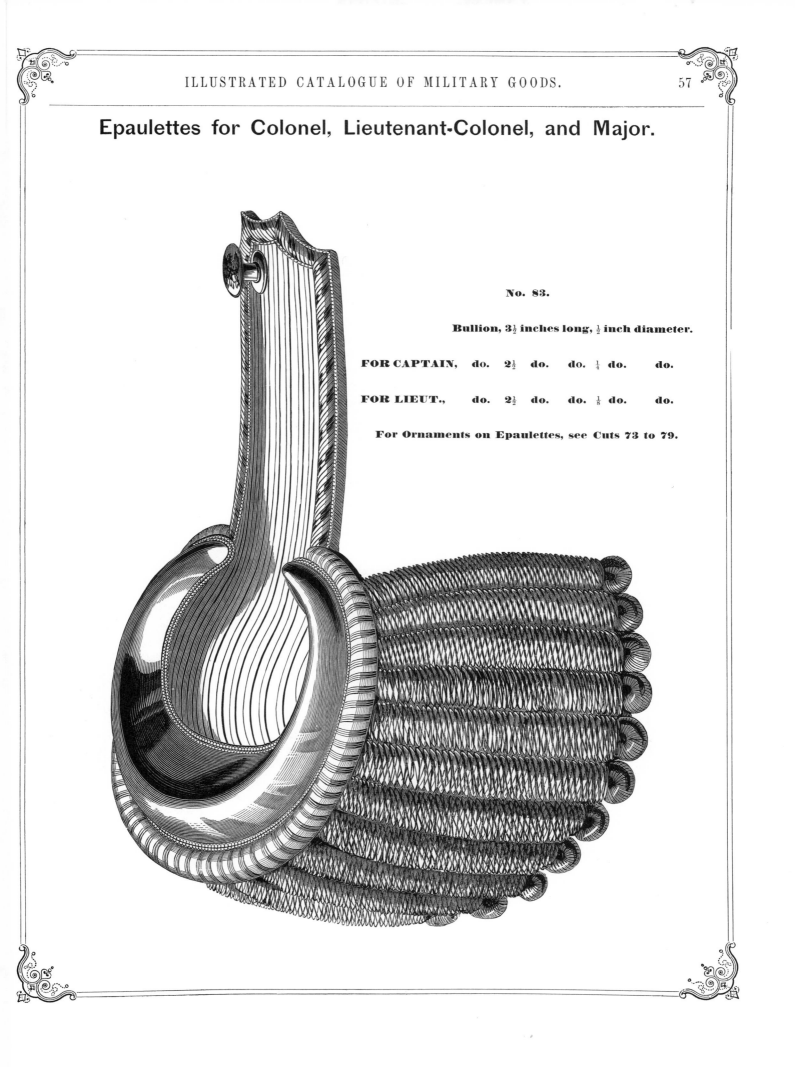

No. 83.

Bullion, 3½ inches long, ½ inch diameter.

FOR CAPTAIN, do. 2½ do. do. ¼ do. do.

FOR LIEUT., do. 2½ do. do. ⅛ do. do.

For Ornaments on Epaulettes, see Cuts 73 to 79.

Shoulder Straps for Officers—Exact Size of U. S. Regulation.

Length of Strap, 4 inches—Width, 1⅜ inches—Width of Embroidery, ¼ inch.
FOR GENERAL STAFF OFFICERS—on Dark Blue Cloth.
FOR INFANTRY, OFFICERS—on Saxony Blue Cloth.
FOR ARTILLERY OFFICERS—on Scarlet Cloth.
FOR RIFLE OFFICERS—on Green Cloth.
FOR CAVALRY OFFICERS—on Yellow Cloth.
FOR DRAGOON OFFICERS—on Orange Cloth.

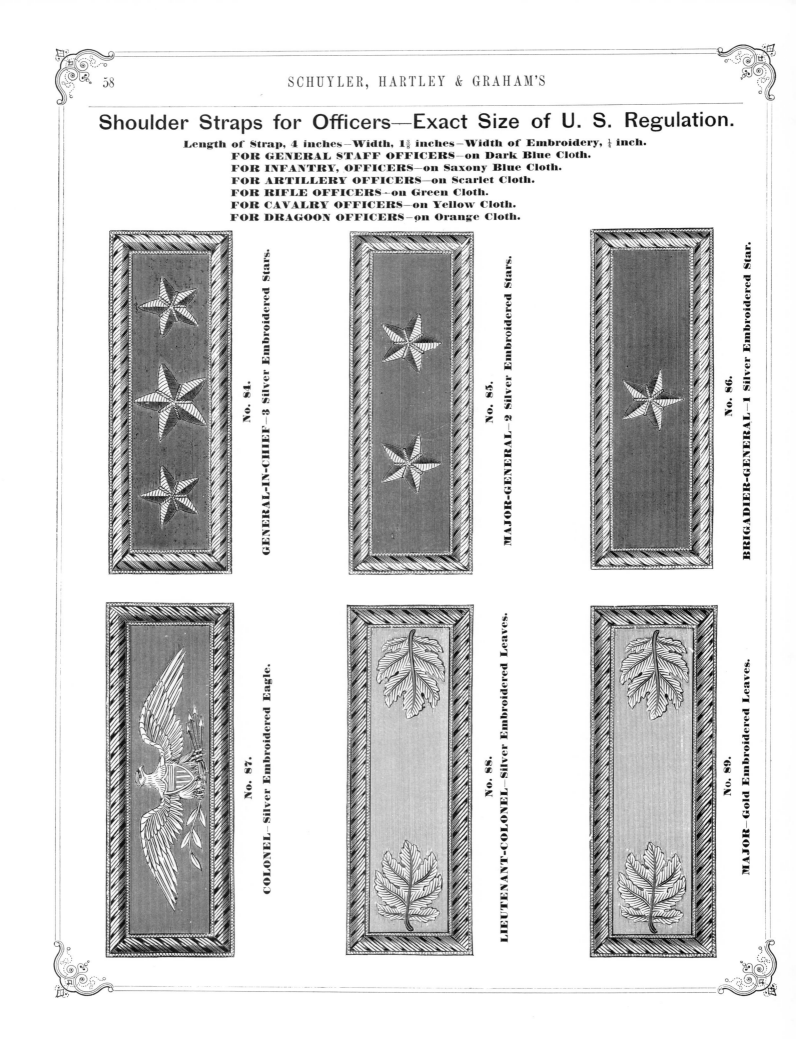

No. 84.
GENERAL-IN-CHIEF—3 Silver Embroidered Stars.

No. 85.
MAJOR-GENERAL—2 Silver Embroidered Stars.

No. 86.
BRIGADIER-GENERAL—1 Silver Embroidered Star.

No. 87.
COLONEL—Silver Embroidered Eagle.

No. 88.
LIEUTENANT-COLONEL—Silver Embroidered Leaves.

No. 89.
MAJOR—Gold Embroidered Leaves.

Shoulder Straps for Officers—Exact Size of U. S. Regulation.

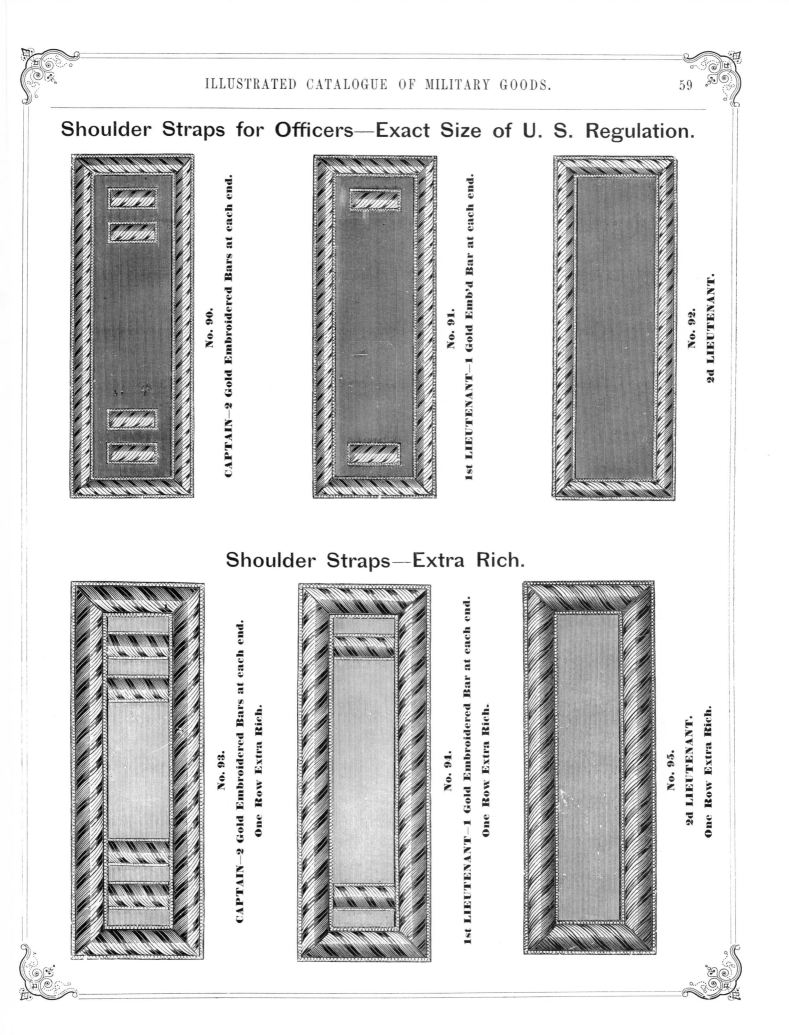

No. 90.
CAPTAIN—2 Gold Embroidered Bars at each end.

No. 91.
1st LIEUTENANT—1 Gold Emb'd Bar at each end.

No. 92.
2d LIEUTENANT.

Shoulder Straps—Extra Rich.

No. 93.
CAPTAIN—2 Gold Embroidered Bars at each end.
One Row Extra Rich.

No. 94.
1st LIEUTENANT—1 Gold Embroidered Bar at each end.
One Row Extra Rich.

No. 95.
2d LIEUTENANT.
One Row Extra Rich.

Miniature Shoulder Straps.

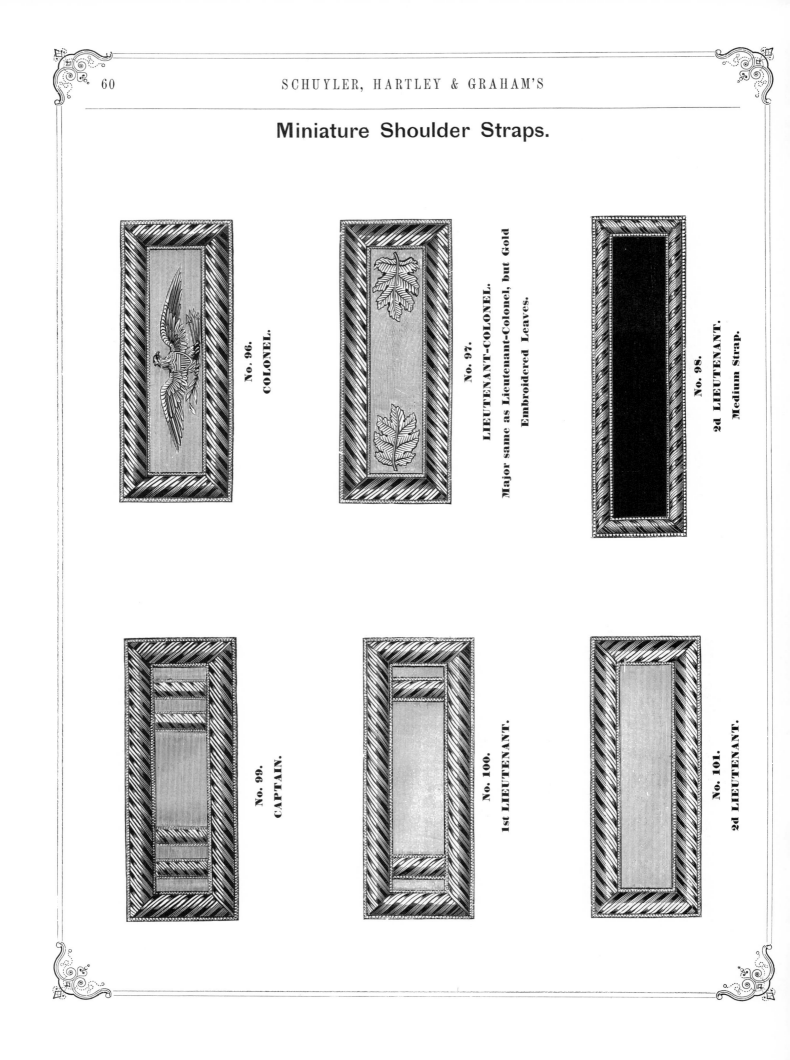

No. 96.
COLONEL.

No. 97.
LIEUTENANT-COLONEL.
Major same as Lieutenant-Colonel, but Gold
Embroidered Leaves.

No. 98.
2d LIEUTENANT.
Medium Strap.

No. 99.
CAPTAIN.

No. 100.
1st LIEUTENANT.

No. 101.
2d LIEUTENANT.

Shoulder Straps.

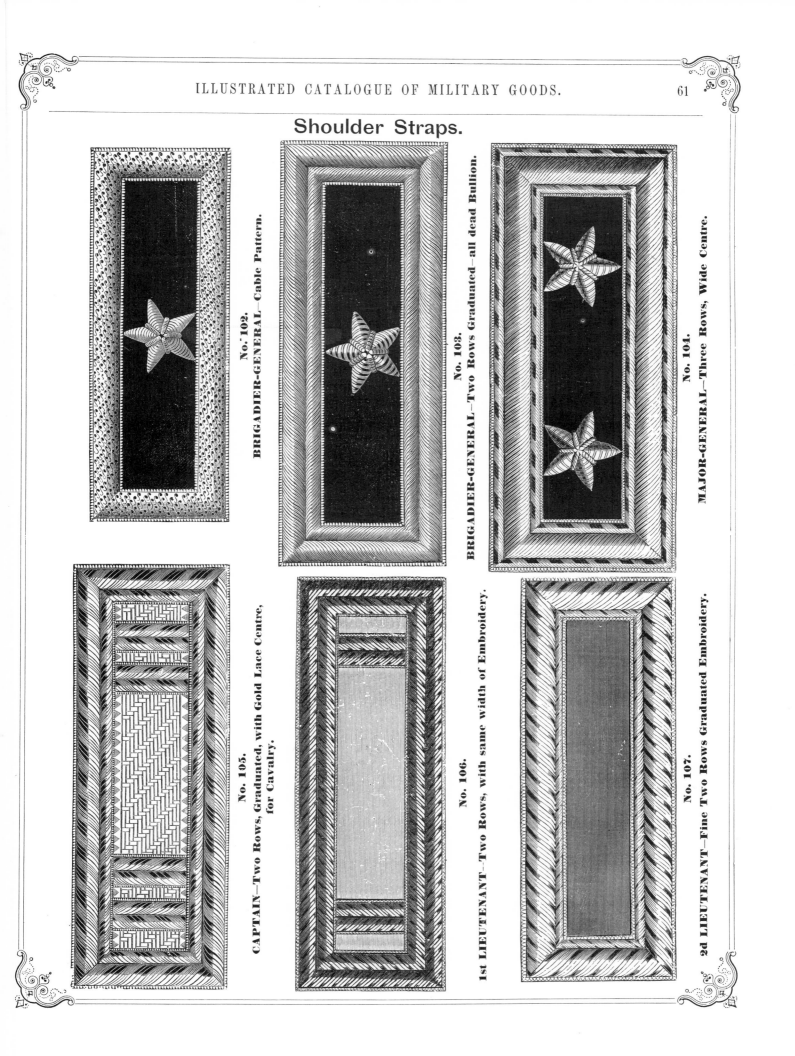

No. 102.
BRIGADIER-GENERAL—Cable Pattern.

No. 103.
BRIGADIER-GENERAL—Two Rows Graduated—all dead Bullion.

No. 104.
MAJOR-GENERAL—Three Rows, Wide Centre.

No. 105.
CAPTAIN—Two Rows, Graduated, with Gold Lace Centre, for Cavalry.

No. 106.
1st LIEUTENANT—Two Rows, with same width of Embroidery.

No. 107.
2d LIEUTENANT—Fine Two Rows Graduated Embroidery.

Extra Rich, Three Row Shoulder Straps, Wide Centre.

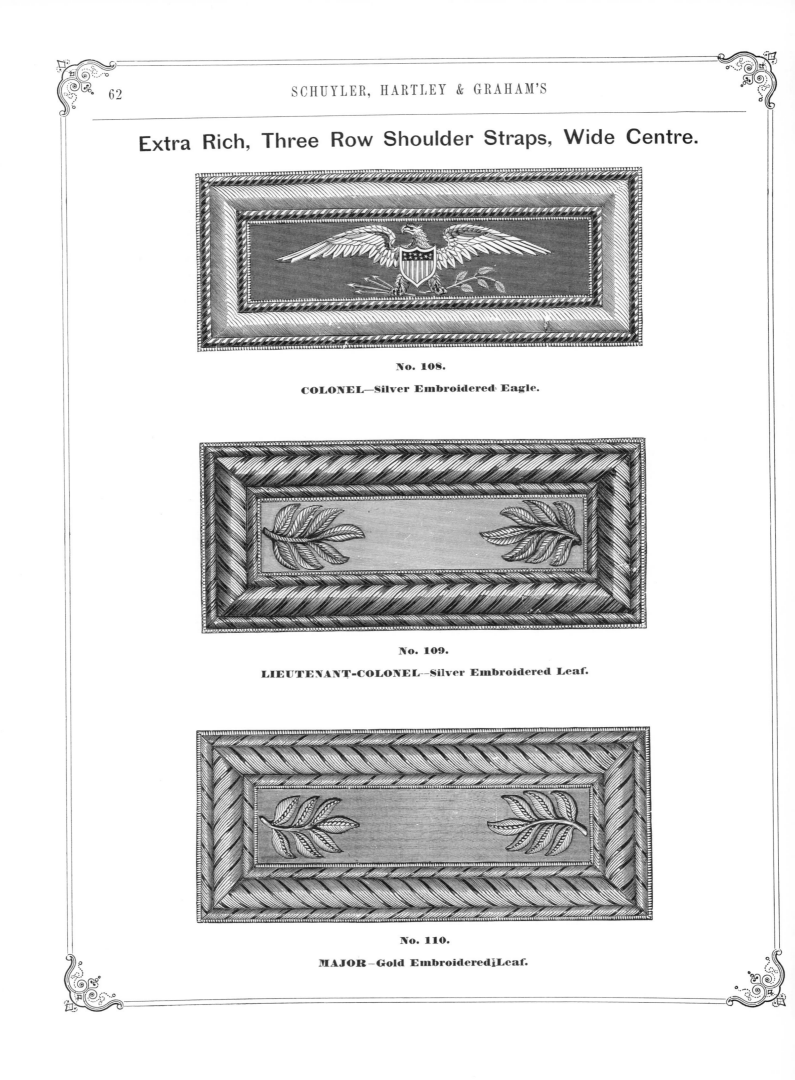

No. 108.

COLONEL—Silver Embroidered Eagle.

No. 109.

LIEUTENANT-COLONEL—Silver Embroidered Leaf.

No. 110.

MAJOR—Gold Embroidered Leaf.

Extra Rich, Three Row Shoulder Straps, Wide Centre.

No. 111.

CAPTAIN—Two Gold Embroidered Bars at each end

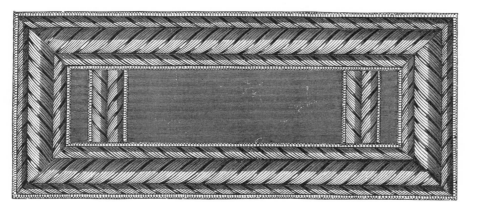

No. 112.

1st LIEUTENANT—One Gold Embroidered Bar at each end.

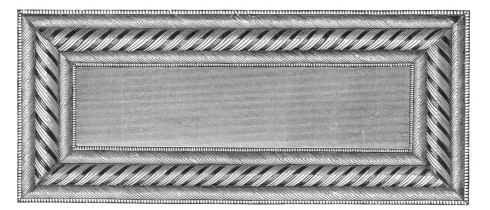

No. 113.

2d LIEUTENANT.

Extra Rich, Three, Four, and Five Row Straps.

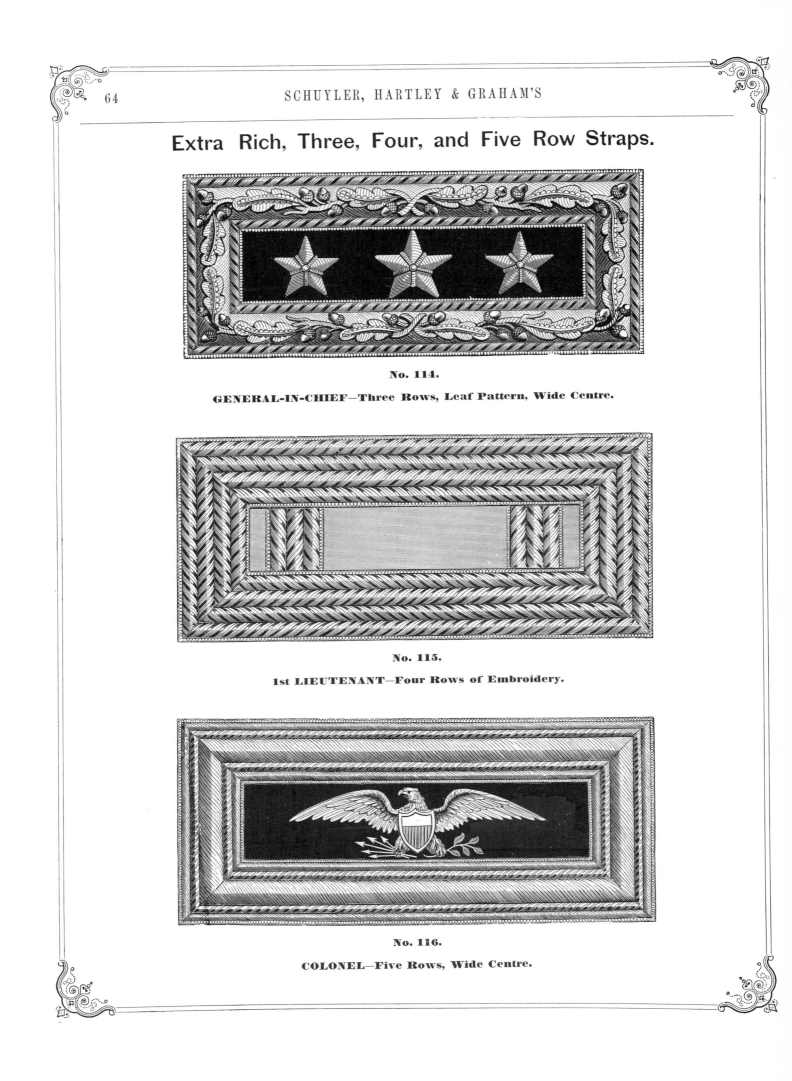

No. 114.

GENERAL-IN-CHIEF—Three Rows, Leaf Pattern, Wide Centre.

No. 115.

1st LIEUTENANT—Four Rows of Embroidery.

No. 116.

COLONEL—Five Rows, Wide Centre.

Embroidered Ornaments.

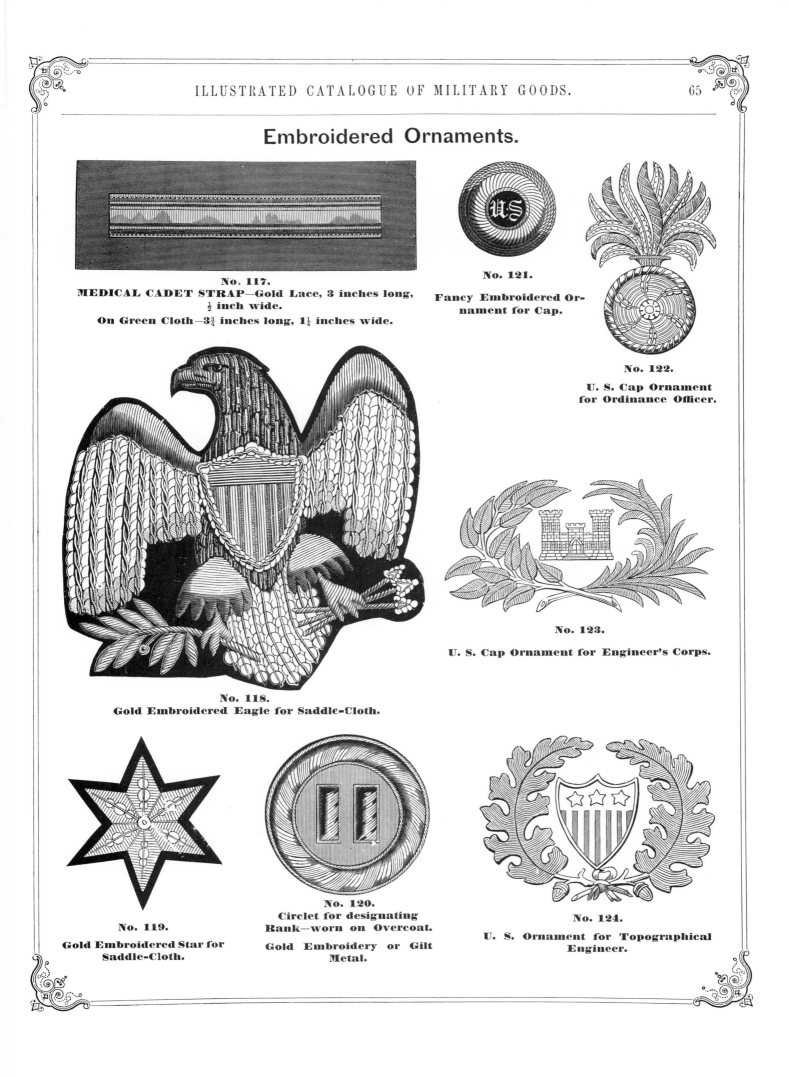

No. 117.
MEDICAL CADET STRAP—Gold Lace, 3 inches long,
½ inch wide.
On Green Cloth—3¾ inches long, 1¼ inches wide.

No. 121.
Fancy Embroidered Or-
nament for Cap.

No. 122.
U. S. Cap Ornament
for Ordinance Officer.

No. 118.
Gold Embroidered Eagle for Saddle-Cloth.

No. 123.
U. S. Cap Ornament for Engineer's Corps.

No. 119.
Gold Embroidered Star for
Saddle-Cloth.

No. 120.
Circlet for designating
Rank—worn on Overcoat.

Gold Embroidery or Gilt
Metal.

No. 124.
U. S. Ornament for Topographical
Engineer.

Hat and Cap Ornaments for Officers.

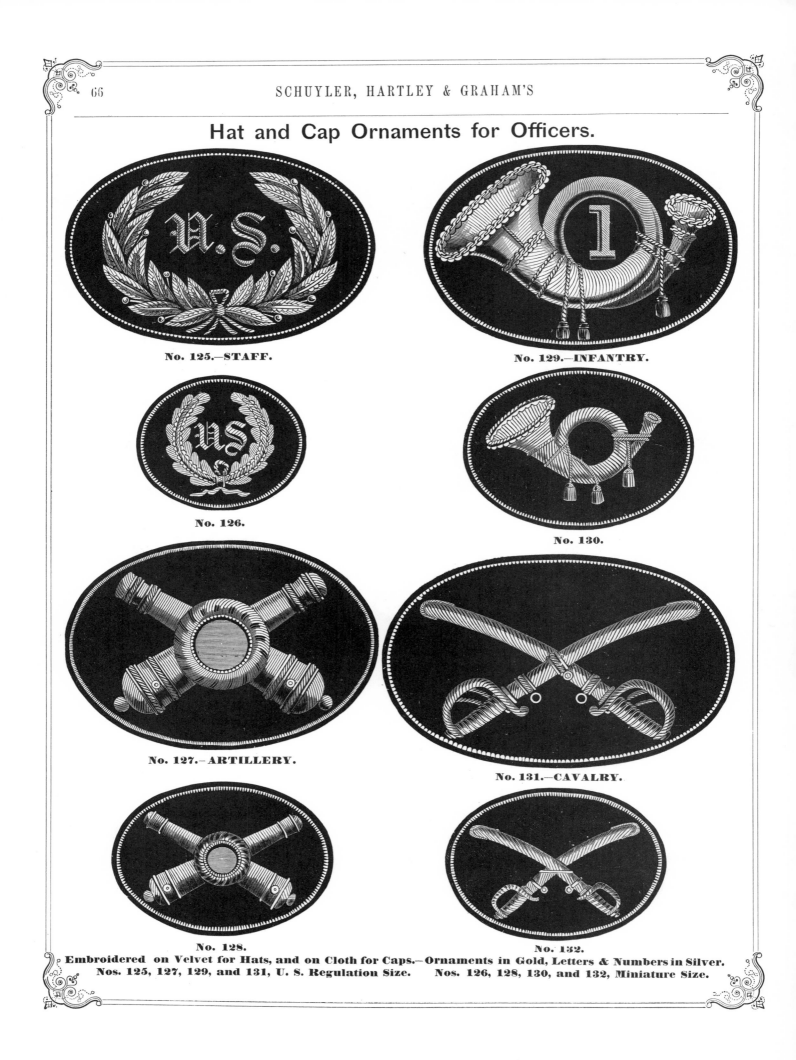

No. 125.—STAFF.

No. 129.—INFANTRY.

No. 126.

No. 130.

No. 127.—ARTILLERY.

No. 131.—CAVALRY.

No. 128.

No. 132.

Embroidered on Velvet for Hats, and on Cloth for Caps.— Ornaments in Gold, Letters & Numbers in Silver.
Nos. 125, 127, 129, and 131, U. S. Regulation Size.   Nos. 126, 128, 130, and 132, Miniature Size.

Trimmings for Coat Sleeves.

No. 133.

Service Chevron—One Enlistment.

No. 134.

Service Chevrons—Two Enlistments.

No. 135.

CORPORAL'S Chevrons

No. 136.

SERGEANT'S Chevrons.

No. 137.

1st SERGEANT.

No. 138.

Ordnance SERGEANT.

No. 139.

QUARTERMASTER'S SERGEANT.

No. 140

SERGEANT-MAJOR.

Badges Worn on Sleeve of Overcoat, to designate Rank.

No. 141.

HOSPITAL STEWARD'S Chevrons—Silk, Embroidered on Green Cloth.

No. 142.

1st LIEUTENANT — One Braid—⅛ inch Black Silk Braid.

No. 143.
CAPTAIN—Two Braids.

No. 144.

MAJOR—Three Braids.

No. 145.

LIEUTENANT-COLONEL— Four Braids.

No. 146.
COLONEL—Five Braids.

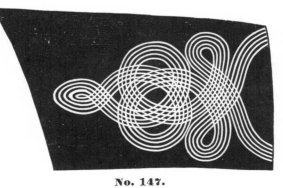

No. 147.
GENERAL—Five Braids.

Army Corps Badges.

No. 148.
1st ARMY CORPS.

No. 149.
2d ARMY CORPS.

No. 150.
3d ARMY CORPS.

No. 151.
5th ARMY CORPS.

No. 152.
6th ARMY CORPS.

No. 153.
11th ARMY CORPS.

No. 154.
12th ARMY CORPS.

1st Division—Red.

2d Division—White.

3d Division—Blue.

Cord, Lace, and Binding.

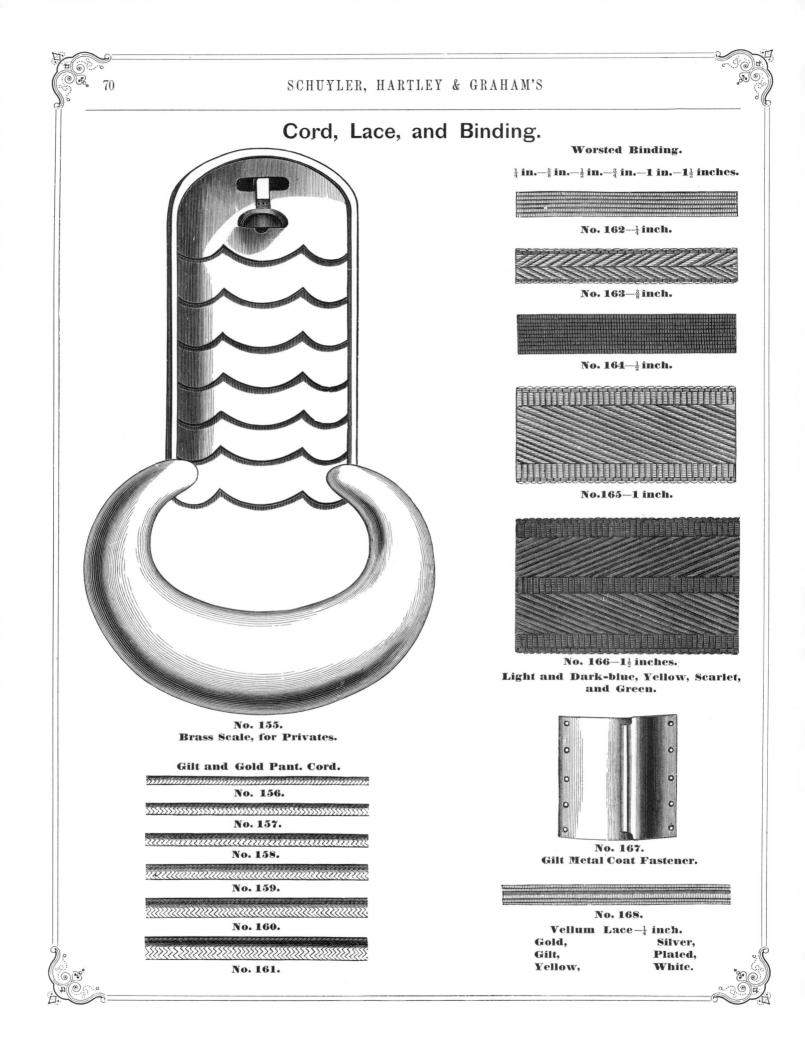

**No. 155.
Brass Scale, for Privates.**

Gilt and Gold Pant. Cord.

No. 156.

No. 157.

No. 158.

No. 159.

No. 160.

No. 161.

Worsted Binding.

¼ in.—⅜ in.—½ in.—¾ in.—1 in.—1½ inches.

No. 162—¼ inch.

No. 163—⅜ inch.

No. 164—½ inch.

No.165—1 inch.

No. 166—1½ inches.
Light and Dark-blue, Yellow, Scarlet,
and Green.

**No. 167.
Gilt Metal Coat Fastener.**

**No. 168.
Vellum Lace—¼ inch.**

Gold,	Silver,
Gilt,	Plated,
Yellow,	White.

U. S. Regulation Buttons.

GENERALS & STAFF.

No. 169.

No 170.

INFANTRY.

No. 171.

No. 172.

ARTILLERY.

No. 173.

No. 174.

CAVALRY

No. 175.

No. 176.

RIFLE.

No. 177.

No. 178.

ENGINEER.

No. 179.

No. 180.

TOPOGRAPHICAL ENGINEER.

NO. 181.

No. 182.

ORDNANCE.

No. 183.

No. 184.

No. 185.
Navy Coat.

No. 186.
Navy Jacket.

No. 187.
Navy Vest.

No. 188.

No. 189.

Shield Button.

No. 190.
Marine Coat.

No. 191.
Marine Jacket.

No. 192.
Marine Vest.

No. 193.

No. 194.

N. Y. State Line Button.

No. 195.
Revenue Coat.

No. 196.
Revenue Jacket.

No. 197.
Revenue Vest.

No. 198.

No. 199.

N. Y. State Staff Button.

Camp Candlesticks, Knives, and Canteens.

View of Upper Section

View of Lower Section

Ready for use.

View of Stick Closed, forming
one pair.

No. 200.
Brass Camp Candlestick.

No. 202.
Cloth Covered Canteen,
with Filter.

No. 201.

Knife, Fork, and Spoon.

No. 203.
Britannia Dram Flasks.
Hog-skin Covered Dram Flasks—Leather Covered do.
¾ Pint—1 Pint—1¼ Pint—1½ Pint.

Spurs—Steel, Brass, Gilt, Plated, and Silver.

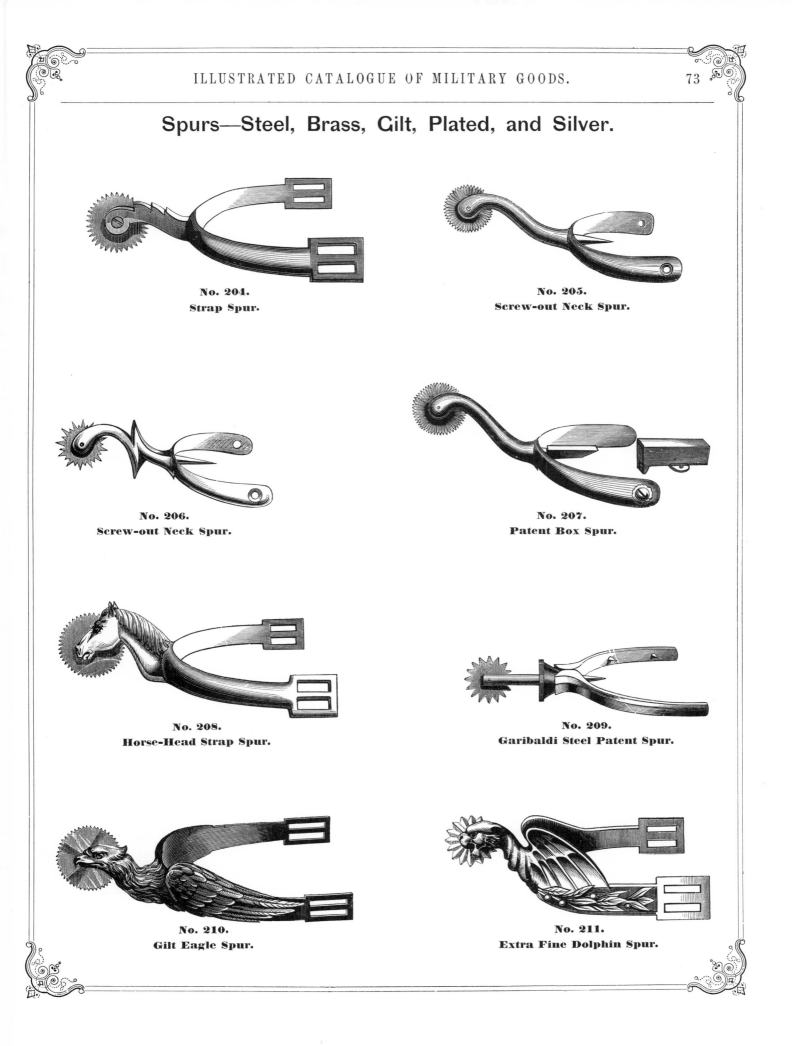

No. 204.
Strap Spur.

No. 205.
Screw-out Neck Spur.

No. 206.
Screw-out Neck Spur.

No. 207.
Patent Box Spur.

No. 208.
Horse-Head Strap Spur.

No. 209.
Garibaldi Steel Patent Spur.

No. 210.
Gilt Eagle Spur.

No. 211.
Extra Fine Dolphin Spur.

Eagles, Spear-heads, Tassels, &c., for Flags.

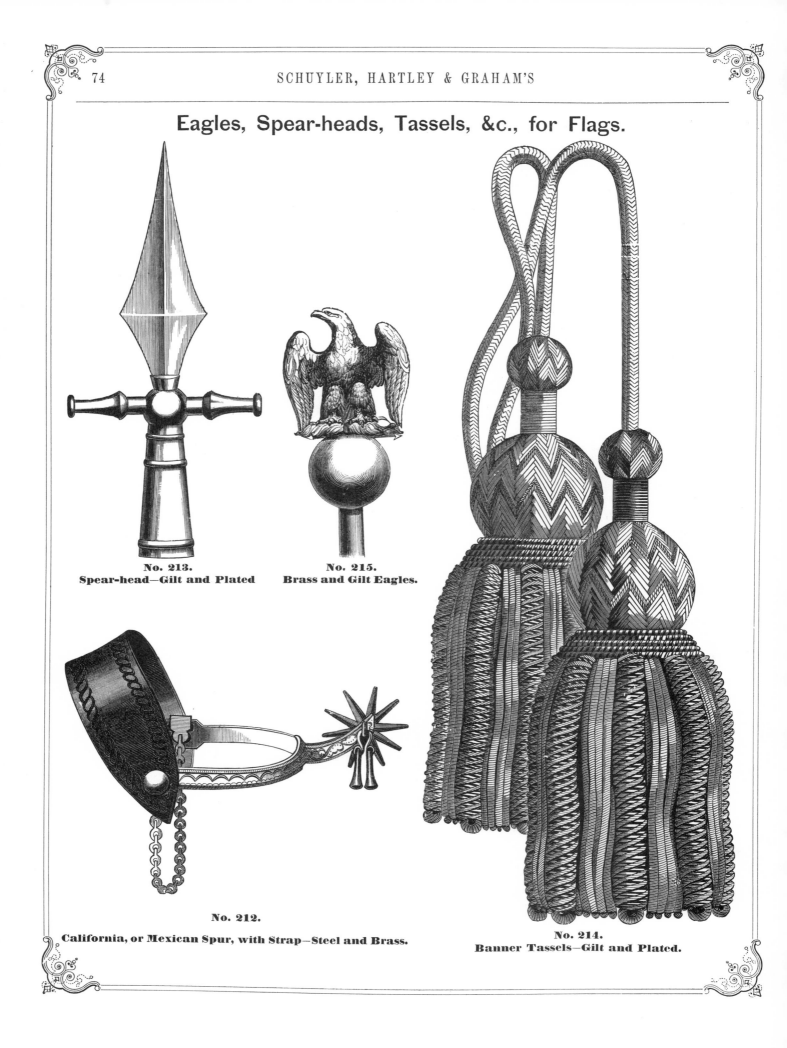

No. 213.
Spear-head—Gilt and Plated

No. 215.
Brass and Gilt Eagles.

No. 212.
California, or Mexican Spur, with Strap—Steel and Brass.

No. 214.
Banner Tassels—Gilt and Plated.

Sash, Foils, Masks, Musical Instruments, &c.

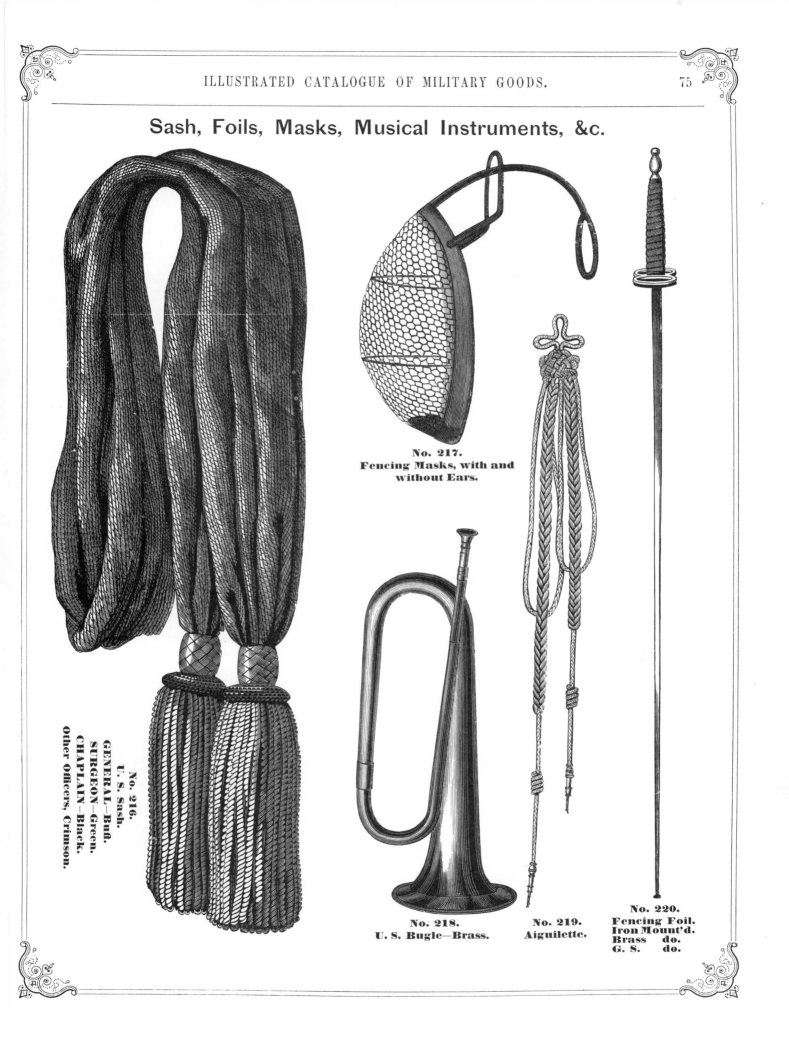

No. 217.
Fencing Masks, with and without Ears.

No. 216.
U. S. Sash.
GENERAL—Buff.
SURGEON—Green.
CHAPLAIN—Black.
Other Officers, Crimson.

No. 218.
U. S. Bugle—Brass.

No. 219.
Aiguilette.

No. 220.
Fencing Foil.
Iron Mount'd.
Brass do.
G. S. do.

Horse Equipments, and Musical Instruments.

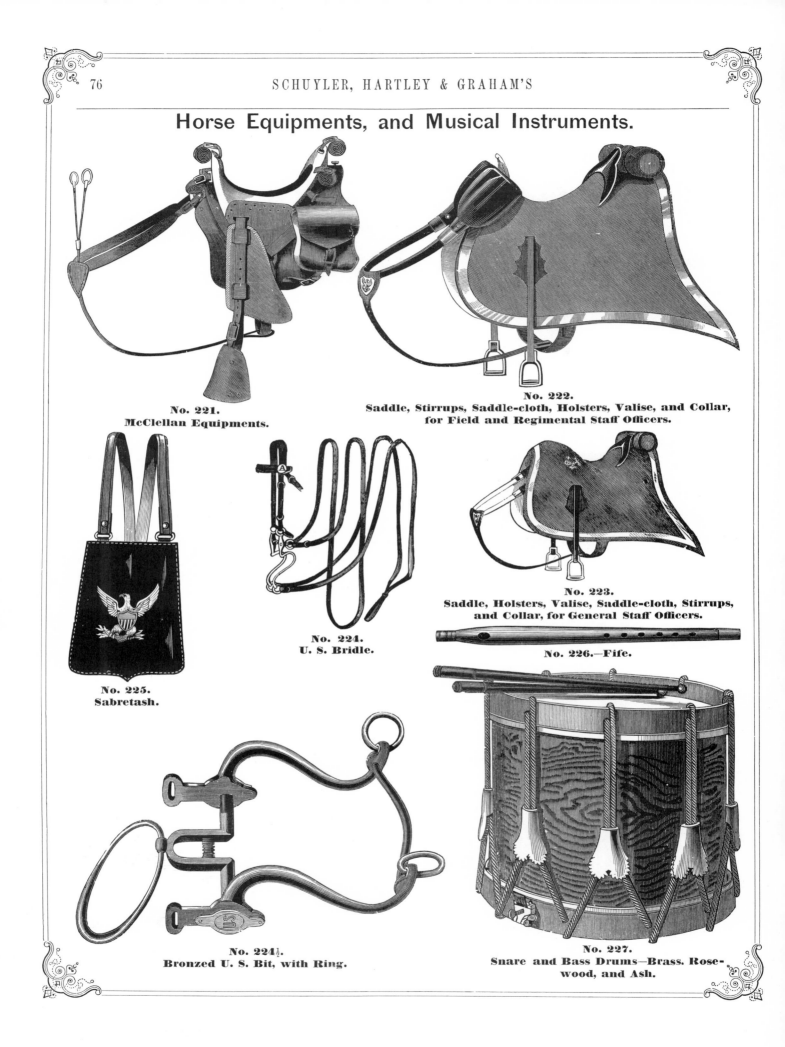

No. 221.
McClellan Equipments.

No. 222.
Saddle, Stirrups, Saddle-cloth, Holsters, Valise, and Collar,
for Field and Regimental Staff Officers.

No. 223.
Saddle, Holsters, Valise, Saddle-cloth, Stirrups,
and Collar, for General Staff Officers.

No. 224.
U. S. Bridle.

No. 226.—Fife.

No. 225.
Sabretash.

No. 224½.
Bronzed U. S. Bit, with Ring.

No. 227.
Snare and Bass Drums—Brass. Rose-
wood, and Ash.

Field Glasses.

No. 228.

Black Japanned, or Leather Covered.

No. 229.—Double Extension.

Gold and Silver Medals.

Reverse   side.

No. 230.

Reverse   side.

No. 231.

Reverse   side

No. 232.
French—Cross of the Legion of Honor.

Reverse   side.

No. 233.
Prussian—Cross of the Crown.

Reverse   side

No. 234.
Roman—Military Cross of St. Gregory.

Reverse   side.

No. 235.
Austrian—Decoration of the Iron Cross.

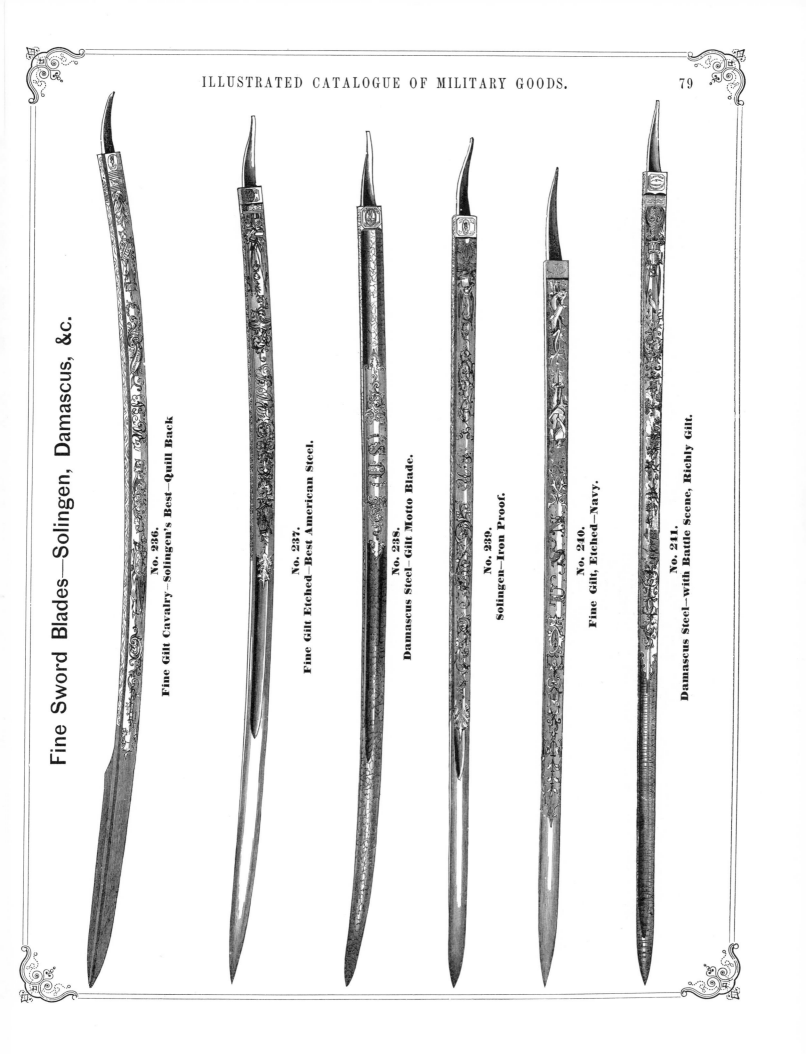

Fine Sword Blades—Solingen, Damascus, &c.

No. 236.
Fine Gilt Cavalry—Solingen's Best—Quill Back

No. 237.
Fine Gilt Etched—Best American Steel.

No. 238.
Damascus Steel—Gilt Motto Blade.

No. 239.
Solingen—Iron Proof.

No. 240.
Fine Gilt, Etched—Navy.

No. 241.
Damascus Steel—with Battle Scene, Richly Gilt.

Sword-Case and Gauntlet.

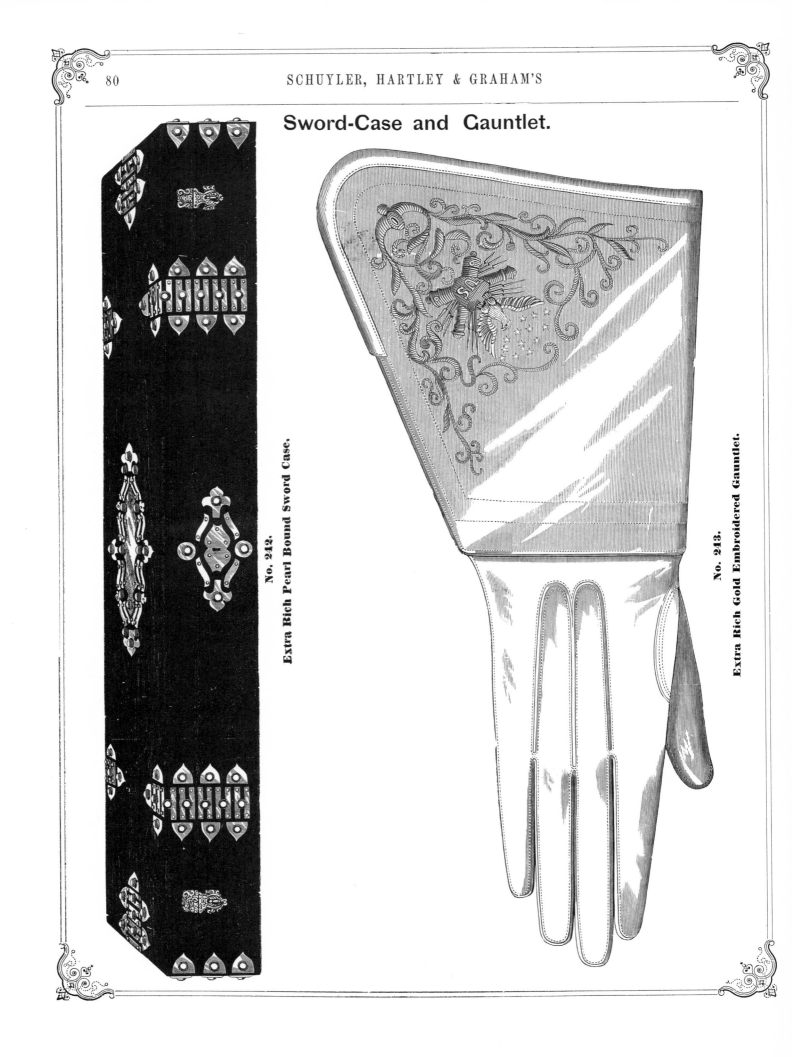

No. 242.

Extra Rich Pearl Bound Sword Case.

No. 243.

Extra Rich Gold Embroidered Gauntlet.

Overcoat Throgs, Braid and Cord.

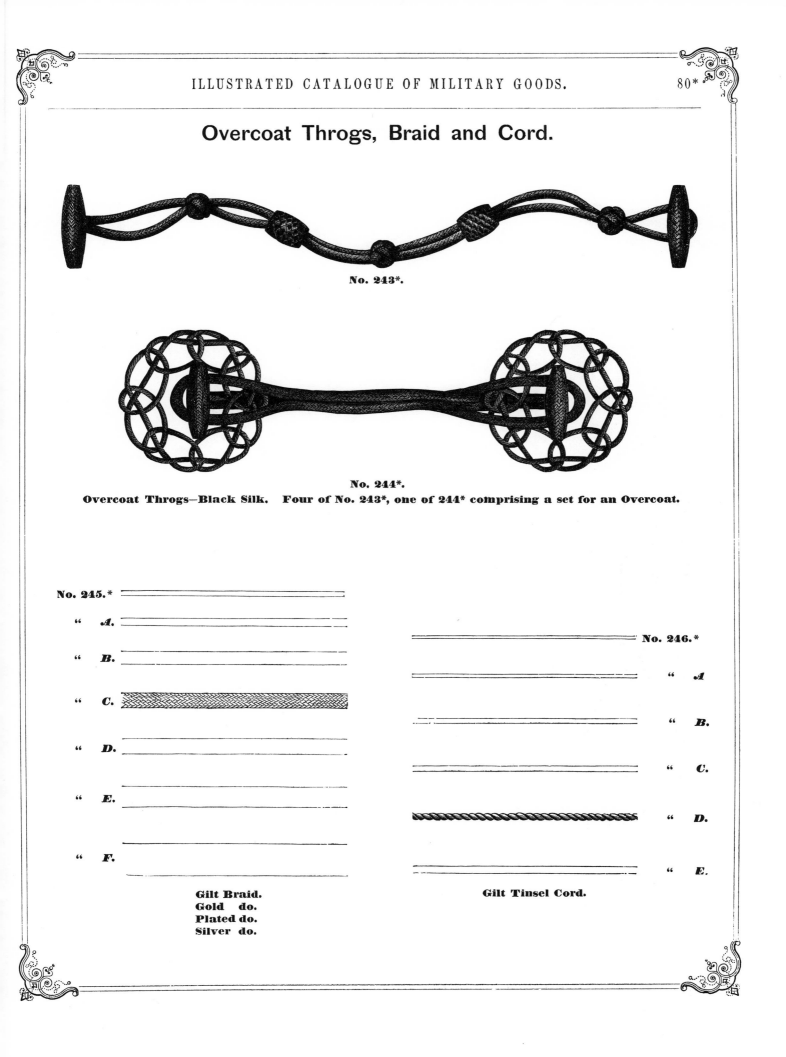

No. 243*.

No. 244*.

Overcoat Throgs—Black Silk.   Four of No. 243*, one of 244* comprising a set for an Overcoat.

No. 245.*

"   *A.*

"   *B.*

"   *C.*

"   *D.*

"   *E.*

"   *F.*

No. 246.*

"   *A*

"   *B.*

"   *C.*

"   *D.*

"   *E.*

Gilt Braid.
Gold   do.
Plated do.
Silver do.

Gilt Tinsel Cord.

REGULATIONS

FOR THE

Uniform and Dress

OF

THE NAVY

Of the United States.

REGULATIONS

FOR THE

Uniform of the Navy of the United States.

GENERAL REGULATIONS.

201. *Full dress.*—Frock coat, epaulettes, cocked hat, sword, and plain pantaloons; the coat to be worn fully buttoned. The epaulettes, cocked hat, and sword-knot are to be dispensed with during the war.

202. *Undress.*—The same as full dress, but without cocked hat or epaulettes, and with or without sword.

203. *Service dress.*—The same as undress. Swords to be worn at quarters and on leaving a navy yard or vessel on duty.

204. *Officers* are to wear their uniform, either full or undress, whenever they make official visits to the President of the United States, the Secretary of the Navy, or to foreign authorities and vessels of war; when acting as members of courts-martial, courts of inquiry, boards of examination, or of special boards, or when attending such boards as witnesses, or in any other capacity.

It is left optional with officers to wear their uniform while on duty in the Navy Department, at the Observatory, or on light-house duty ashore.

205. *Uniform* is to be worn by all officers when attached to any vessel of the navy or Coast Survey, to any navy yard or station, or to any hospital or other naval establishment, for duty, unless when absent on leave.

206. *Officers on furlough* will not wear their uniform, and officers are strictly prohibited from wearing any part of it while suspended from duty by sentence of a court-martial.

207. *On all occasions of ceremony*, abroad or in the United States, when a commanding officer may deem it necessary to order the attendance of the officers under his command, he shall be careful in such order to prescribe the particular dress to be worn.

208. *Officers* attached to vessels of the United States Navy in foreign ports will not visit the shore without being in uniform.

209. *Officers* appointed on "temporary service" are not required to supply themselves with full-dress uniforms, but are required to obtain undress uniforms and side-arms.

210. *Officers* holding executive appointments in the volunteer service of the navy are to wear the same uniform as is authorized for their respective grades in the regular service.

211. Before a vessel proceeds to sea, there will be a general muster for the purpose of ascertaining whether the officers and crew are provided with the uniform prescribed by the regulations, and the commanding officer of the vessel will see that all deficiencies are supplied.

COATS.

212. *For a Rear-Admiral, Commodore, Captain, Commander, Lieutenant-Commander, Lieutenant, Master,* and *Ensign,* and all *Staff Officers* of assimilated rank, respectively, to be as follows:

Frock coat, of navy-blue cloth, faced with the same, and lined with black silk serge; double breasted, with two rows of large navy buttons on the breast, nine in each row, placed four inches and a half apart from eye to eye at top, and two inches and a half at bottom; rolling collar; skirts to be full, commencing at the hip bone and descending four-fifths thence towards the knee, with one button behind on each hip and one near the bottom of each fold; cuffs to be closed and from two and a half to three inches deep.

213. *For gunners, boatswains, carpenters,* and *sailmakers,* the same.

214. *For midshipmen, third assistant engineers,* and *clerks,* the same, except that the buttons are to be of medium size only.

215. *For a master's mate,* receiving $40 per month, frock coat, of navy-blue cloth or flannel; rolling collar; single breasted, with nine navy buttons of medium size on the breast, one behind on each hip, one near the bottom on each fold, and none on the cuffs. They will also wear a gold star above the cuff, and the navy cap, with simply the wreath.

216. *For masters' mates,* receiving $25 per month, *yeomen, masters-at-arms, sergeants, stewards,* and *paymasters' stewards,* blue cloth or flannel jacket, rolling collar, double breasted, with two rows of medium sized navy buttons on the breast, six in each row; and slashed sleeves, with four small sized navy buttons. They will also wear the navy cap without wreath or device.

OVERCOATS.

217. Shall be a caban overcoat and cape, of dark blue beaver or pilot-cloth, lined throughout with dark blue flannel; skirt to extend four inches below the knee; cape to be ten inches shorter; double breasted, with pockets in side seam, and buttons arranged as for frock coat; the cape to be made so that it can be removed at pleasure, and provided with an extra cloth collar to detach, so as to form a separate garment. On each end of the collar of the overcoat shall be the following devices: For a Rear-Admiral two silver stars; Commodore, one silver star; Captain, a silver eagle; Commander, a silver leaf; Lieutenant-Commander, a gold leaf; Lieutenant, two silver bars; Master, one silver bar; Ensign, a small gold cord on the front edge of the collar. Staff officers of corresponding assimilated rank are to wear the same designations. Stars, eagle, and bars to be parallel to the ends of the collar. The overcoats of *all other officers* than those above mentioned are to have no devices, and but seven buttons in each row.

JACKETS.

218. *Jackets* may be worn as "service dress" by all officers, except at general muster, or upon special occasions of ceremony, when a different dress is prescribed by the commanding officer; to be of navy-blue cloth or navy-blue fine flannel, faced with the same, and lined with black silk serge; double or single breasted, as in the coat; rolling collar, with the same number of small sized buttons on the breast as for the coat, and with the same arrangement of lace on the cuffs, and the same shoulder straps.

219. In mild climates or seasons officers in "service dress" may wear the uniform made of navy-blue fine flannel. Coats to be lined with black silk serge, and furnished with navy buttons of medium size. The same may be worn on shipboard at sea, except at general muster; also on board ship in port, except at general muster, when on watch with the colors hoisted, or on occasions of ceremony, when a different dress is prescribed by the commanding officer.

CUFF AND SLEEVE ORNAMENTS.

220. The lace on the cuffs and sleeves is to be navy gold lace, a quarter of an inch wide, and to be placed a quarter of an inch apart, except where a half is hereinafter designated, the first strip being below but joining the cuff seam, and the others distributed in groups upwardly.

221. *For a Rear-Admiral*, eight strips, with half an inch space between first and second, fourth and fifth, and seventh and eighth.

222. *For a Commodore*, seven strips, with half an inch space between third and fourth, fourth and fifth.

223. *For a Captain*, six strips, with half an inch space between third and fourth.

224. *For a Commander*—five strips, with half an inch space between first and second, fourth and fifth.

225. *For a Lieutenant-Commander*, four strips, with half an inch space between third and fourth.

226. *For a Lieutenant*, three strips; for a *Master*, two strips; and for an *Ensign*, one strip.

227. On the upper side of each sleeve, above the lace and midway the seams, is to be worn a star of five rays, embroidered in gold, and one inch in diameter, with one of its rays directly downwards, the point thereof being a quarter of an inch from the upper edge of the lace.

228. *For a midshipman, boatswain, gunner*, and *master's mate*, at $40 per month, the star without the lace, and in the same position as the star on the sleeves of an ensign.

229. The cuff and sleeve ornaments of the *staff officers* are to be the same as for the *line officers* with whom they assimilate, respectively, in rank, except the gold star, which is to be worn by *line officers* only.

230. No other officers are entitled to the ornaments above described.

PANTALOONS

231. *For all officers*, to be of navy-blue cloth or white drill, or for "service dress" of navy-blue fine flannel, and to be worn over the boots or shoes.

232. Within the tropics, white pantaloons are to be worn at all seasons, unless when otherwise authorized by the officer in command.

233. *North* of the tropics blue ones are to be worn from the 1st of October to the 15th of May, and white ones from the 15th of May to the 1st of October; and *south* of the tropics *vice versa*, subject, however, to such exceptions as may be directed or authorized by the senior officer present in command.

VESTS.

234. *For all officers*, single breasted, standing collar, with nine small navy buttons in front.

SHOULDER STRAPS.

235. All shoulder straps, except for gunners, boatswains, carpenters, and sailmakers, are to be of navy-blue cloth, four inches and a quarter long, and one inch and a half wide, including the border, which is to be a quarter of an inch wide, and embroidered in gold.

236. The centre and end ornaments, or distinctions of the line and staff, and indications of rank, are to be embroidered in gold or in silver, as hereinafter designated, and are to be as follows :

237. *Line officers.*—For a *Rear-Admiral*—a silver foul anchor in the centre, in a horizontal position, and a silver star of five rays at each end.

238. *For a Commodore*—a silver star, embroidered on a gold foul anchor, in the centre.

239. *For a Captain*—a silver spread eagle, resting on a silver plain anchor, in the centre.

240. *For a Commander*—a silver foul anchor in the centre, and a silver oak leaf at each end.

241. *For a Lieutenant-Commander*—a silver foul anchor in the centre, and a gold oak leaf at each end.

242. *For a Lieutenant*—a silver foul anchor in the centre, and two gold bars at each end.

243. *For a Master*—a silver foul anchor in the centre, and a gold bar at each end.

244. *For an Ensign*—a silver foul anchor in the centre.

245. *Staff officers* are to wear shoulder straps of the same description as prescribed for *line officers* with whom they assimilate, respectively, in rank, with the following exceptions as to centre devices :

246. In the *Medical Corps*, the anchor is omitted; in the *Paymasters' Corps*, an oak sprig, in silver is substituted; in the *Engineer Corps*, a device of four oak leaves, in silver, in the form of a cross, is substituted; for *Professors of Mathematics*, the letter 𝔓, in silver relief, on plain gold circle, is substituted; for *Naval Constructors*, a live-oak sprig is substituted; for *Chaplains*, a silver cross is substituted; for *Secretaries*, the letter 𝔖, in silver, is substituted.

247. *Midshipmen, Third Assistant Engineers*, and *Clerks*, are not to wear straps.

248. *Gunners, boatswains, carpenters*, and *sailmakers*, are to have shoulder straps of plain gold lace, four inches long, and three-quarters of an inch wide, the *boatswain* to have the letter 𝔅, and the *carpenter* the letter ℭ, embroidered in silver, midway upon their straps.

249. For the exact dimensions and form of the devices, and the manner of arranging them, see plates, by which the officers will be guided.

CAP AND CAP ORNAMENTS.

250. *Cap*—of dark blue cloth; top to be one-half inch greater diameter than the base; quarters one and a half inch wide between the seams; back of the band to be two inches wide between the points of the visor, with a welt half an inch from the lower edge, extending from point to point of the visor; band in front one and a half inch wide; bound, black patent leather visor, green underneath, two and a half inches wide, and rounded, as per pattern; inside of the band of heavy duck. The cap ornaments are to be worn on the band in front. During rainy weather a black cover may be worn over the cap.

251. *Cap ornaments* shall consist of a gold wreath in front, composed of oak and olive branches, three inches in width, and inclosing the following described devices:

252. *For a Rear-Admiral*—two silver stars, each five-eighths of an inch in diameter, with their centres four-fifths of an inch apart.

253. *For a Commodore, Captain, Commander, Lieutenant-Commander, Lieutenant, Master,* and *Ensign*—a silver foul anchor, seven-eighths of an inch long, in a vertical position.

254. *For Medical Officers*—an oak leaf, in silver, nine-tenths of an inch long, in a vertical position.

255. *For Paymasters*—an oak sprig, composed of three leaves, in silver, nine-tenths of an inch in height, in a vertical position.

256. *For Engineers*—four oak leaves, in silver, in the form of a cross, one and one-tenth of an inch horizontally, and nine-tenths of an inch vertically.

257. *For Naval Constructors*—a sprig, composed of two leaves of live-oak, in silver, in a vertical position, and with a spread of one and one-fourth of an inch.

258. *For Chaplains*—a silver cross, seven-eighths of an inch in length, and one-half an inch in width, in an oblique position.

259. *For Professors of Mathematics*—the letter *P*, in silver, and in relief upon a plain gold circle, four-fifths of an inch in diameter.

260. *For Secretaries*—the letter *S*, in silver, one-half an inch in length.

261. *For all other officers*—simply the wreath.

262. For more minute descriptions of the devices, and the manner of arranging them, see drawings.

STRAW HATS.

263. In tropical climates, or during warm seasons, officers may wear white straw hats, under the same restrictions as in the case of jackets; the body of the hat to be not more than four and a half nor less than four inches in height, and the rim not more than three and a half nor less than three inches in width, with a plain band of black ribbon.

SWORD AND SCABBARD.

264. *For all officers*—shall be a cut-and-thrust blade, not less than twenty-six nor more than twenty-nine inches long; half-basket hilt; grip, white. Scabbards of black leather; mountings of yellow gilt, and all as per pattern.

SWORD-BELT.

265. *For all officers*—shall be of plain black glazed leather, not less than one inch and a half nor more than two inches wide, with slings of the same not less than one-half nor more than three-quarters of an inch wide, and a hook in the forward ring to suspend the sword. Belt-plate of yellow gilt in front, two inches in diameter, as per pattern. The belt to be worn over the coat.

BUTTONS.

266. Shall be gilt, convex, and of three sizes in exterior diameter: large, seven-eighths of an inch; medium, seven-tenths of an inch; and small, nine-sixteenths of an inch. Each size is to have the same device. See drawings.

CRAVAT.

267. *For all officers*—to be of black silk or satin, with a white shirt collar showing above it.

DRESS FOR PETTY OFFICERS AND CREW.

268. *Boatswain's mates, gunner's mates, carpenter's mates, sailmaker's mates,* and *ship's cook,* will wear, embroidered in white silk, on the right sleeve of their blue jackets, above the elbow in front, an eagle and anchor, of not more than three inches in length, with a star of one inch in diameter, one inch above. The same device, embroidered in blue, to be worn on the sleeves of their white frocks in summer.

369. *All other petty officers,* except officers' stewards, will wear the same device on their left sleeves.

270. The outside clothing for *petty officers, firemen,* and *coal-heavers, seamen, ordinary seamen, landsmen,* and *boys,* for muster, shall consist of blue cloth jackets and trowsers, or blue woolen frocks; black hats; black silk neckerchiefs, and shoes, or boots in cold weather. In warm weather it shall consist of white frocks and trowsers; black or white hats, as the commander may for the occasion direct, having proper regard for the comfort of the crew; black silk neckerchiefs, and shoes; the collars and cuffs to be lined with blue cotton cloth, and stitched round with thread. Thick blue cloth caps, without visors, may be worn by the crew at sea, except on holidays or at muster.

271. It is strictly enjoined upon commandants of stations and commanding officers of the navy to see that the foregoing regulations are complied with in every respect, and to require all deviations from them to be corrected.

GIDEON WELLES,
Secretary of the Navy.

Navy Department, *January* 28, 1864.

NAVY OFFICERS' PAY TABLE.

Grades.	Pay per annum.
REAR-ADMIRALS (Active List.)	
When at sea	$5,000
When on shore duty	4,000
On leave or waiting orders	3,000
On Retired List	2,000
COMMODORES, (Active List.)	
When at sea	4,000
When on shore duty	3,200
On leave or waiting orders	2,400
On Retired List	1,800
CAPTAINS, (Active List.)	
When at sea	3,500
When on shore duty	2,800
On leave or waiting orders	2,100
On Retired List	1,600
COMMANDERS, (Active List.)	
When at sea	2,800
When on shore duty	2,240
On leave or waiting orders	1,680
On Retired List	1,400
LIEUTENANT-COMMANDERS, (Active List.)	
When at sea	2,343
When on shore duty	1,875
On leave or waiting orders	1,500
On Retired List	1,300
LIEUTENANTS (Active List.)	
When at sea	1,875
When on shore duty	1,500
On leave or waiting orders	1,200
On Retired List	1,000

Grades.	Pay per annum.
MASTERS, (Active List.)	
When at sea	$1,500
When on shore duty	1,200
On leave or waiting orders	960
On Retired List	800
ENSIGNS, (Active List.)	
When at sea	1,200
When on shore duty	960
On leave or waiting orders	768
On Retired List	500
MIDSHIPMEN	500
FLEET SURGEONS	3,300
SURGEONS—	
On duty at sea—	
For first five years after date of commission as surgeon	2,200
For second five years after date of commission as surgeon	2,400
For third five years after date of commission as surgeon	2,600
For fourth five years after date of commission as surgeon	2,800
For twenty years and upwards after date of commission	3,000
On other duty—	
For first five years after date of commission as surgeon	2,000
For second five years after date of commission as surgeon	2,200
For third five years after date of commission as surgeon	2,400

Grades.	Pay per annum.
For fourth five years after date of commission as surgeon	$2,600
For twenty years and upwards after date of commission . . .	2,800
On leave or waiting orders—	
For first five years after date of commission as surgeon	1,600
For second five years after date of commission as surgeon . . .	1,800
For third five years after date of commission as surgeon	1,900
For fourth five years after date of commission as surgeon . . .	2,100
For twenty years and upwards after date of commission	2,300

RETIRED SURGEONS—

Surgeons ranking with Captains .	1,300
Surgeons ranking with Commanders .	1,100
Surgeons ranking with Lieutenants	1,000

RETIRED PASSED AND ASSISTANT SURGEONS—

Passed	850
Assistant	650

PASSED ASSISTANT SURGEONS—

On duty at sea	1,500
On other duty	1,400
On leave or waiting orders . . .	1,100

ASSISTANT SURGEONS—

On duty at sea	1,250
On other duty	1,050
On leave or waiting orders . .	800

PAYMASTERS—

On duty at sea—

For first five years after date of commission	2,000
For second five years after date of commission	2,400
For third five years after date of commission	2,600
For fourth five years after date of commission	2,900
For twenty years and upwards after date of commission	3,100

On other duty—

Grades.	Pay per annum.
For first five years after date of commission	$1,800
For second five years after date of commission	2,100
For third five years after date of commission	2,400
For fourth five years after date of commission	2,600
For twenty years and upwards after date of commission . . .	2,800

On leave or waiting orders—

For first five years after date of commission	1,400
For second five years after date of commission . . . . ,	1,600
For third five years after date of commission	1,800
For fourth five years after date of commission	2,000
For twenty years and upwards after date of commission	2,250

PAYMASTERS RETIRED—[Under Acts of Aug. 3, and Dec. 21, 1861.]

Paymasters ranking with Captain . .	1,300
Ranking with Commanders . .	1,100
Ranking with Lieutenants . . .	1,000

ASSISTANT PAYMASTERS—

On duty at sea—

First five years after date of commission	1,300
After five years from date of commission	1,500

On other duty—

First five years after date of commission	1,000
After five years from date of commission	1,200

On leave or waiting orders—

First five years after date of commission	800
After five years from date of commission	1,000

CHAPLAINS—To be paid as Lieutenants.

PROFESSORS OF MATHEMATICS—

On duty	1,800
On leave or waiting orders . . .	960

Grades.	Pay per annum.
BOATSWAINS, GUNNERS, CARPENTERS, AND SAILMAKERS—	
On duty at sea—	
For first three years' sea-service from date of appointment* . . .	$1,000
For second three years' sea-service from date of appointment . . .	1,150
For third three years' sea-service from date of appointment . . .	1,250
For fourth three years' sea-service from date of appointment . . .	1,350
For twelve years' sea-service and upwards	1,450
On other duty—	
For first three years' sea-service after date of appointment . . .	800
For second three years' sea-service after date of appointment . . .	900
For third three years' sea-service after date of appointment . . .	1,000
For fourth three years' sea-service after date of appointment . . .	1,100
For twelve years' sea-service and upwards	1,200
On leave or waiting orders—	
For first three years' sea-service after date of appointment . . .	600
For second three years' sea-service after date of appointment . . .	700
For third three years' sea-service after date of appointment . . .	800
For fourth three years' sea-service after date of appointment . . .	900
For twelve years' sea-service and upwards	1,000
ENGINEERS—	
CHIEF ENGINEERS, (on duty)—	
For first five years after date of commission	1,800
For second five years after date of commission	2,200
For third five years after date of commission	2,450

* Act of July 16, 1862.

Grades.	Pay per annum.
After fifteen years from date of commission	$2,600
On leave or waiting orders—	
For first five years after date of commission	1,200
For second five years after date of commission	1,300
For third five years after date of commission	1,400
After fifteen years from date of commission	1,500
FIRST ASSISTANT ENGINEERS—	
On duty	1,250
On leave or waiting orders . .	900
SECOND ASSISTANT ENGINEERS—	
On duty	1,000
On leave or waiting orders . .	750
THIRD ASSISTANT ENGINEERS—	
On duty	750
On leave or waiting orders . .	600
NAVY AGENTS, commissions not to exceed	3,000
NAVY AGENT at San Francisco . .	4,000
TEMPORARY NAVY AGENTS .	
NAVAL STOREKEEPERS . . .	
Officers of the navy on foreign stations	1,500
ENGINEER-IN-CHIEF . . .	3,000
NAVAL CONSTRUCTORS . . .	2,600
NAVAL CONSTRUCTORS, when not on duty	1,800
SECRETARIES to commanders of squadrons	1,500
CLERKS to commanders of squadrons and commanders of vessels . . .	500
At navy yards Portsmouth, N. H., and Philadelphia	900
At navy yard Mare Island . .	1,500
At all other navy yards* . . .	1,200
FIRST CLERKS to commandants—	
At Mare Island	1,500
At all other navy yards . . .	1,200

✿ Act of July 16, 1862.

Grades.	Pay per annum.
SECOND CLERKS to commandants—	
At Boston and New York . . .	$960
At Washington	960
CLERKS—	
To paymasters in ships-of-the-line .	700
To paymasters in frigates . .	500
To paymasters in smaller vessels than a frigate	400
To paymasters at navy yards . .	750
To inspectors in charge of provisions, &c.	750

Grades.	Pay per month
YEOMEN—	
In 1st rates	$45
In 2d rates	40
In 3d rates	30
In 4th rates	24
ARMORERS—	
In 1st rates	30
In 2d rates	25
In 3d rates	20
MATES—	
Master's (acting)	40
Boatswain's	25
Gunner's	25
Carpenter's	25
Sailmaker's	20
Armorer's	20
MASTER-AT-ARMS	25
SHIP'S CORPORALS	20
COXSWAINS	24
QUARTERMASTERS	24
QUARTER GUNNERS . .	20

Grades.	Pay per month
CAPTAINS—	
Of forcastle	$24
Of tops	20
Of afterguard	20
Of hold	20
COOPERS	20
PAINTERS	20
STEWARDS—	
Officer's	20
Surgeon's, of 1st or 2d rates . .	40
Surgeon's, of 3d rates . . .	33
Surgeon's, of 4th rates . . .	25
Paymaster's, of 1st, 2d, and 3d rates	33
Paymaster's, of 4th rates . . .	30
NURSES—	
Where complement is less than 200, one nurse (3d and 4th rates) .	14
Where complement is over 200, two nurses, each (1st and 2d rates) .	14
COOKS—	
Ship's	24
Officer's	20
MASTERS OF THE BAND . .	20
MUSICIANS—	
First class	15
Second class	12
SEAMEN	18
ORDINARY SEAMEN . . .	14
LANDSMEN	12
BOYS	8, 9 & 10
FIREMEN—	
First class	30
Second class	25
COAL-HEAVERS	18

NOTES.—All officers, while at sea or attached to a sea-going vessel, shall be allowed one ration.

No rations shall be allowed to any officers of the navy on the retired list.

The pay of all naval officers appointed by virtue of an act, entitled, "An act to provide for the temporary increase of the navy," approved July 24, 1861, shall be the same as that of officers of a like grade in the regular navy.—(See act July 16, 1862.)

Organization of the Navy Department.
JANUARY 1, 1864.

OFFICE OF THE SECRETARY OF THE NAVY.

NAME.	DUTY.	PLACE OF BIRTH.	WHERE A CITIZEN.	DATE OF ORIGINAL APPOINTMENT.	SALARY.
Gideon Welles	Secretary	Conn	Conn	7 Mar., 1861	$8,000
Gustavus V. Fox	Assistant Secretary.	Mass	Mass	9 May, 1861	4,000
William Faxon	Chief Clerk	Conn	Conn	19 Mar., 1861	2,200
Wm. Plume Moran	Clerk	Va	Va	8 Dec., 1852	1,800
Do.	Disbursing Clerk				200
George S. Watkins	Clerk	Tenn	Tenn	1 Jan., 1854	1,600
John W. Hogg	do	Penn	D, C	12 July, 1843	1,600
Walter S. McNairy	do	Tenn	Tenn	28 May, 1852	1,600
Francis H. Stickney	do	Maine	Maine	29 May, 1861	1,600
Holmes E. Offley	do	D. C	D. C	1 Aug., 1861	1,600
Charles P. Thompson	do	Va	D. C	6 Sept., 1861	1,400
Henry H. Tilley	do	R. I	R. I	1 Aug., 1861	1,400
Charles Faxon	do	N. Y	Ill	3 Feb., 1863	1,400
Charles R. Knowles	do	N. Y	N. Y	1 Aug., 1863	1,400
George Alvord	do	Conn	Conn	1 Jan., 1863	1,200
James A. Sample	do	Ind	Ind	15 Ap'l, 1862	1,200
Silas P. Wrisley	do	Vt	Mass	5 May, 1863	1,200
Jesse E. Dow	do	D. C	D. C	8 May, 1863	1,200
Elisha Risley	do	Conn	Conn	28 July, 1863	1,200
Harrison S. Bowen	Messenger	D. C	D. C	6 June, 1862	900
Lindsay Muse	Assistant Messenger	Va	D. C	1 Jan., 1829	700

BUREAU OF YARDS AND DOCKS.

NAME.	DUTY.	PLACE OF BIRTH.	WHERE A CITIZEN.	DATE OF ORIGINAL APPOINTMENT.	SALARY.
Joseph Smith	Chief of Bureau	Mass	Mass	25 May, 4846	$4,000
Wm. P. S. Sanger	Civil Engineer	Mass	D. C	15 Sept., 1842	3,000
John W. Bronaugh	Chief Clerk	Va	D. C	4 June, 1849	1,800
Augustus E. Merritt	Clerk	Conn	Conn	10 July, 1857	1,400
Milton B. Cushing	do	N. Y	N. Y	28 Aug. 1861	1,400
William E. Wall	do	N. Y	N. Y	26 Aug., 1862	1,400
Houghton Wheeler	do	N. Y	N. Y	15 Jan., 1863	1,200
Charles Gordon	Draughtsman	Mass	D. C	18 April, 1861	1,400
Charles Huntt	Messenger	Mass	D. C	12 July, 1843	840

BUREAU OF NAVIGATION.

NAME.	DUTY.	PLACE OF BIRTH.	WHERE A CITIZEN.	DATE OF ORIGINAL APPOINTMENT.	SALARY.
Charles Henry Davis	Chief of Bureau	Mass	Mass	17 July, 1862	$4,000
Benjamin F. Greene	Chief Clerk	N. H	N. Y	19 Feb., 1863	1,800
James B. T. Tupper	Clerk	Mass	Mass	12 Sept., 1863	1,200
Henry Dahle	Messenger	Md	D. C	8 May, 1862	840

BUREAU OF ORDNANCE.

NAME.	DUTY.	PLACE OF BIRTH.	WHERE A CITIZEN.	DATE OF ORIGINAL APPOINTMENT.	SALARY.
Henry A. Wise	Chief of Bureau, *ad interim*	N. Y	N. Y	25 June, 1863	$3,500
Richmond Aulick	Assistant	Conn	Va	25 June, 1863	3,000
C. E. Graves	Chief Clerk	Vt	Vt	9 Aug., 1861	1,800
J. D. Brandt	Clerk	S. C	D. C	1 July, 1863	1,600
Charles C. Burr	do	Conn	Conn	18 June, 1858	1,400
S. T. Ellis	do	Penn	D. C	1 July, 1863	1,400

BUREAU OF ORDNANCE, (CONTINUED.)

NAME.	DUTY.	PLACE OF BIRTH.	WHERE A CITIZEN.	DATE OF ORIGINAL APPOINTMENT.	SALARY.
Frank Buttrick	Clerk	Mass	Mich	14 July, 1863	$1,400
Charles K. Stellwagen	Draughtsman.	Penn	Penn	1 Oct., 1849	1,400
Oliver C. Fisher	Messenger	England	N. Y	1 April, 1862	840

BUREAU OF EQUIPMENT AND RECRUITING.

NAME.	DUTY.	PLACE OF BIRTH.	WHERE A CITIZEN.	DATE OF ORIGINAL APPOINTMENT.	SALARY.
Albert N. Smith	Chief of Bureau, *ad interim*	Maine	Mass	30 May, 1863	$3,500
S. Henriques	Chief Clerk	Sweden	N. Y	2 Sept., 1862	1,800
Wm. W. S. Dyre	Clerk	Mass	Penn	21 Oct., 1862	1,400
Baron Proctor	do	Vt	Mo	1 Ap'l, 1863	1,400
James G. Kinne	do	Conn	Conn	1 Jan., 1863	1,200
James W. Dyre	do	Mass	Penn	23 Ap'l, 1863	1,200
Monroe Dilley	Messenger	Penn	Penn	30 July, 1863	840

BUREAU OF MEDICINE AND SURGERY.

NAME.	DUTY.	PLACE OF BIRTH.	WHERE A CITIZEN.	DATE OF ORIGINAL APPOINTMENT.	SALARY.
William Whelan	Chief of Bureau	Penn	Penn	1 Oct., 1853	$3,500
Phineas J. Horwitz	Asst. to Bureau	Md	Penn	3 June, 1859	2,800
Chester Tuttle	Clerk	Penn	Penn	7 July, 1853	1,400
Wythe Denby	do	Va	Ky	9 July, 1860	1,400
Marsh B. Clark	Messenger	Penn	Penn	1 Sept., 1842	840

BUREAU OF PROVISIONS AND CLOTHING.

NAME.	DUTY.	PLACE OF BIRTH.	WHERE A CITIZEN.	DATE OF ORIGINAL APPOINTMENT.	SALARY.
Horatio Bridge	Chief of Bureau	Maine	Maine	1 Oct., 1854	$3,500
Thomas Fillebrown	Chief Clerk	Maine	Maine	1 Sept., 1842	1,800
Lucius B. Allyn	Clerk	Conn	Conn	15 Aug., 1848	1,400
Edward C. Eddie	do	N. Y	Mich	28 Oct., 1853	1,400
Charles Sedgwick	do	N. Y	N. Y	25 Feb., 1862	1,400
Wm. H. Allyn	do	Conn	Wis	9 Jan., 1863	1,400
Edward A. Birnie	do	Md	N. Y	1 Ap'l, 1863	1,400
C. C. Bishop	do	Maine	Mass	9 July, 1863	1,400
George Rye	do	Md	Va	1 Aug., 1861	1,200
Wm. A. Elliott	do	Md	Md	1 July, 1858	1,200
Thomas B. Cockle	do	N. Y	N. Y	1 Dec., 1863	1,200
William Lucas	Messenger	D. C	D. C	6 Aug., 1861	840

BUREAU OF CONSTRUCTION AND REPAIR.

NAME.	DUTY.	PLACE OF BIRTH.	WHERE A CITIZEN.	DATE OF ORIGINAL APPOINTMENT.	SALARY.
John Lenthall	Chief of Bureau	D. C	Penn	18 Nov., 1853	$3,500
A. B. Farwell	Chief Clerk	Maine	Maine	20 April 1861	1,800
A. G. Alden	Clerk	N. H	Wis	3 Ap'l, 1861	1,400
James W. Deeble	do	D. C	D. C	6 Ap'l, 1861	1,400
G. W. Smith	do	N. Y	Md	27 Ap'l, 1861	1,400
William G. Ridgely	do	D. C	D. C	18 Feb., 1861	1,400
F. N. Blake	do	Maine	Kansas	1 Ap'l, 1862	1,400
A. Rothwell	do	Penn	D. C	6 Feb., 1863	1,200
Richard Powell	Draughtsman	Penn	Penn	1 Nov., 1849	1,400
John Sauerwein	Messenger	Germany	Conn	29 Ap'l, 1861	840

BUREAU OF STEAM ENGINEERING.

NAME.	DUTY.	PLACE OF BIRTH.	WHERE A CITIZEN.	DATE OF ORIGINAL APPOINTMENT.	SALARY.
Benj. F. Isherwood	Chief of Bureau	N. Y	N. Y	25 July, 1862	$3,500
Edward B. Neally	Chief Clerk	Maine	Iowa	17 Ap'l, 1861	1,800
George B. Whiting	Draughtsman	N. Y	D. C	18 May, 1863	1,400
Morris Botticher	Asst. Draughtsman,	Prussia	D. C	1 July, 1863	1,200
A. S. Wight	Messenger	Maine	D. C	26 July, 1862	840

NAVY ILLUSTRATIONS.

Navy Swords.

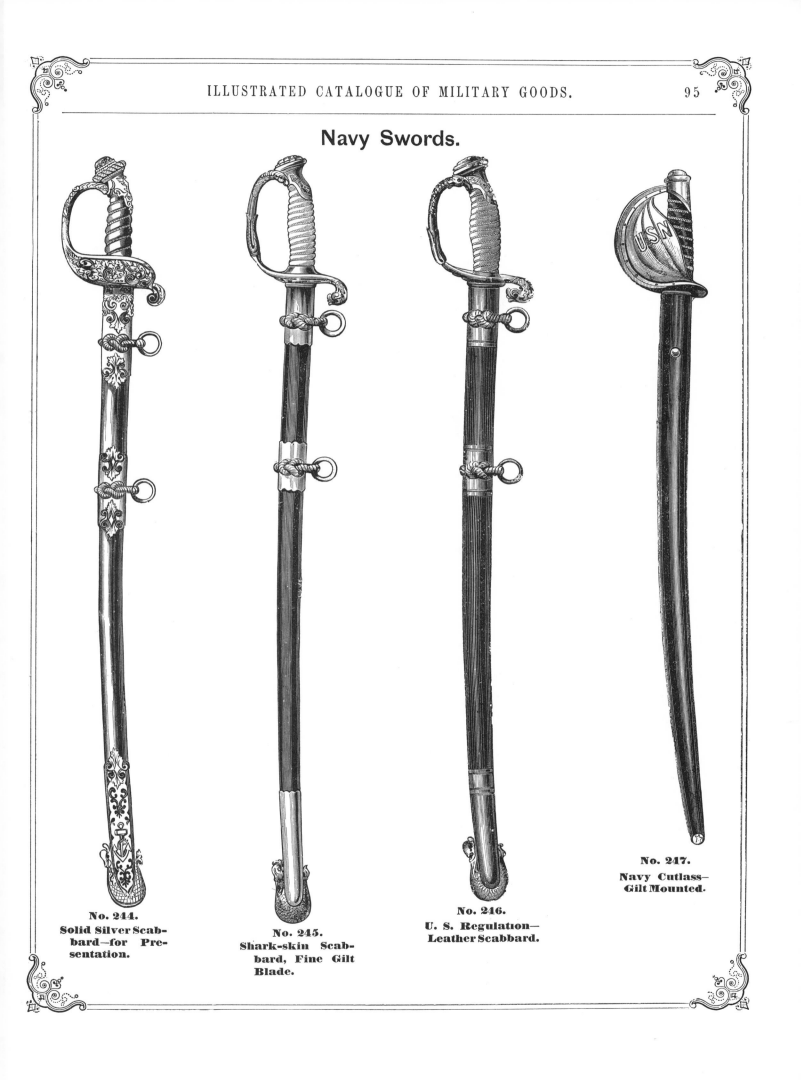

No. 244.
Solid Silver Scabbard—for Presentation.

No. 245.
Shark-skin Scabbard, Fine Gilt Blade.

No. 246.
U. S. Regulation—Leather Scabbard.

No. 247.
Navy Cutlass—Gilt Mounted.

Navy Sword Knots.

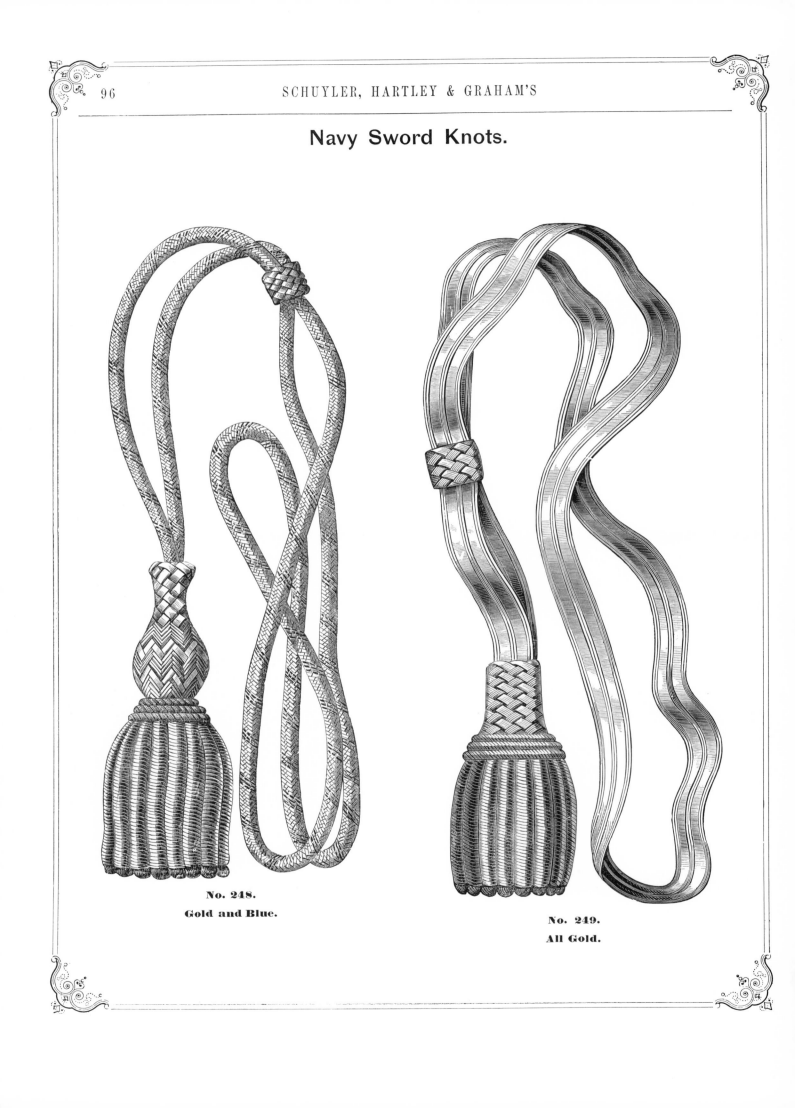

No. 248.

Gold and Blue.

No. 249.

All Gold.

NAVAL CAP ORNAMENTS.

Width of Wreaths 3 in.

ADMIRAL.

Nº 256.

Diameter of Stars $\frac{5}{8}$ of an in.
Betwⁿ centers " " $\frac{4}{5}$ " " "

Commodore, Captain, Commander, Lieut. Commander, Lieutenant, Master and Ensign.

Nº 257.

Length of Anchor $\frac{7}{8}$ᵗʰˢ "

SURGEON.

Nº 258.

Length of Leaf $\frac{9}{10}$ᵗʰˢ "

PAYMASTER.

Nº 259.

Height of Center Ornament $\frac{9}{10}$ᵗʰ "

CHAPLAIN.

Nº 260.

Length of Cross $\frac{7}{8}$ᵗʰˢ "
Width " " $\frac{1}{2}$ in.

ENGINEER.

Nº 261.

Length of Centre Ornament 1 $\frac{4}{10}$ᵗʰ "
Height " " " $\frac{9}{10}$ "

PROFESSOR.

Nº 262.

Diameter of Circle $\frac{4}{5}$ᵗʰˢ "
with letter raised in relief.

CONSTRUCTOR.

Nº 263.

Spread of live oak leaves 1 $\frac{1}{4}$ in.

SECRETARY.

Nº 264.

FOR OTHER OFFICERS.

Nº 265.

ADMIRAL.

No. 266. 4¼ *Anchor in length ⅞.*
Stars in diam.r ⅞.
From center of Star to end of Strap ⅞.
Width of Border ¼ in.

COMMODORE.

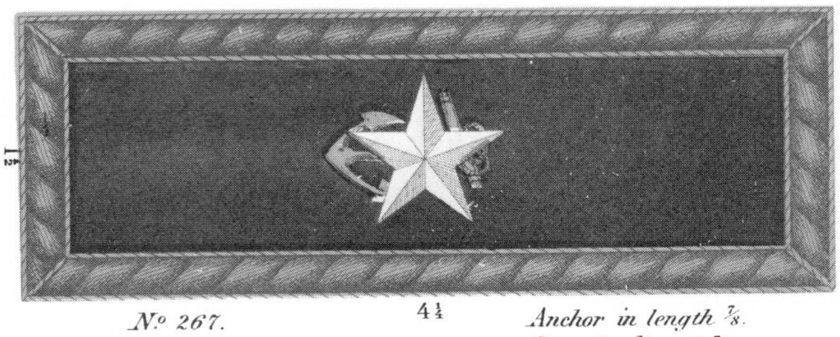

No. 267. 4¼ *Anchor in length ⅞.*
Star in diam.r ⅞.

CAPTAIN.

No. 268. 4¼

COMMANDER.

No. 269. 4¼ *Leaf in length ⅝.*
Stalk of leaf from end of Strap ⅜.
Length of Anchor ⅞.

LIEUTENANT COMMANDER.

No. 270. 4¼ *Leaf in length ⅝.*
Stalk of leaf from end of Strap 2/8.
Length of Anchor ⅞.

LIEUTENANT.

No. 271. 4¼ *Bars 2/10ths wide, ½ in. long.*
" 4/10ths from end to Strap.
Space between bars 1/10th
Anchor ⅞ths long.

MASTER.

No. 272. 4¼ *Bar 2/10ths wide, ½ in. long.*
" 4/10 " from end of Strap.
Anchor ⅞ths long.

ENSIGN.

No. 273. 4¼ *Anchor in length ⅞ths*

CHIEF OF BUREAU OF PROV.ⁿ & CLOTHING.

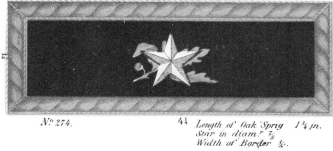

N.º 274.   4¼   Length of Oak Sprig 1¼ in.
Star in diam.ʳ ⅞.
Width of Border ½.

CHIEF OF BUREAU OF CONSTRUCTION.

N.º 275.   Spread of live oak leaves 1²⁄₁₀.
Star in diam.ʳ ⅞.

FLEET PAYMASTERS & PAYMASTER AFTER 15 YEARS.

N.º 276.   Eagle from tip to tip 2 in.
Length of Oak Sprig 1¹⁄₁₀.ᵗʰ

NAVAL CONSTRUCTORS OF MORE THAN 20 YEARS.

N.º 277.   Eagle 2 in. from tip to tip.
Length of live oak sprig ⁹⁄₁₀.ᵗʰˢ

PAYMASTERS, AFTER 1.ˢᵀ FIVE YEARS.

N.º 278.   Length of Oak Sprig 1¼.
End leaf in length ⅝.
Stalk of leaf from end of strap ⅜.

NAVAL CONSTRUCTORS OF MORE THAN 12 YEARS.

N.º 279.   Spread of live oak leaves 1¹⁄₁₀.ᵗʰ
End leaf in length ⅜.
Stalk of leaf from end of Strap ⅜.

PAYMASTERS, 1.ˢᵀ FIVE YEARS.

N.º 280.   Length of Oak Sprig 1¼.
End leaf in length ⅝.
Stalk of leaf from end of Strap ⅜.

NAVAL CONSTRUCTORS OF LESS THAN 12 YEARS.

N.º 281.   Spread of live oak leaves 1¹⁄₁₀.ᵗʰ
End leaf in length ⅜.
Stalk of leaf from end of Strap ⅜.

ASSISTANT PAYMASTER.

N.º 282.   Length of Oak Sprig 1¼.
Bar ²⁄₁₀.ᵗʰ wide, ½ in. long.
  ⁴⁄₁₀.ᵗʰ from end of Strap.

ASSIST NAVAL CONSTRUCTOR.

N.º 283.   Spread of live oak leaves 1¹⁄₁₀.ᵗʰ
Bar ²⁄₁₀.ᵗʰ wide, ½ in. long.
  ⁴⁄₁₀. " from end of Strap.

CHIEF OF BUREAU OF MEDICINE & SURGERY.

No. 284. 4¼ *Star in diam.r 7/8. Width of Border 1/4.*

FLEET SURGEONS & SURGEONS AFTER 15 YEARS.

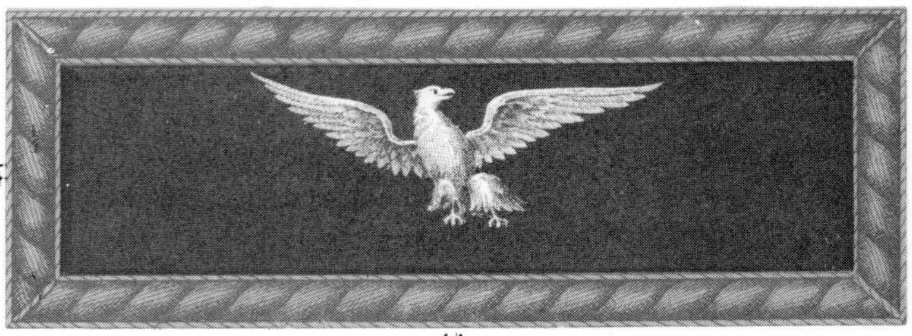

No. 285. 4¼ *Eagle 2 in. from tip to tip.*

SURGEONS AFTER 1ST FIVE YEARS.

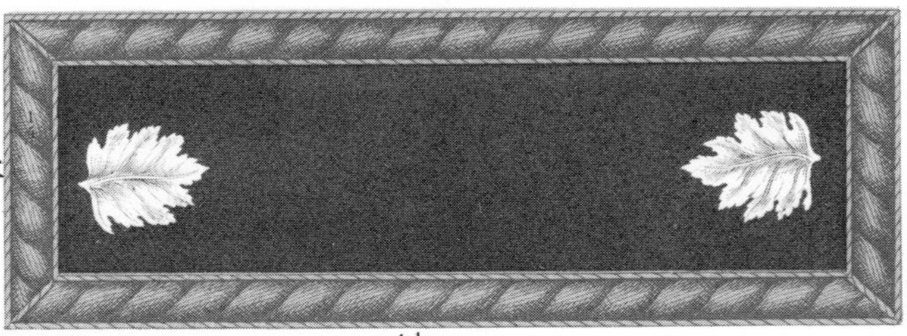

No. 286. 4¼ *Leaf in length 5/8. Stalk of leaf from end of Strap 3/8.*

SURGEONS 1ST FIVE YEARS.

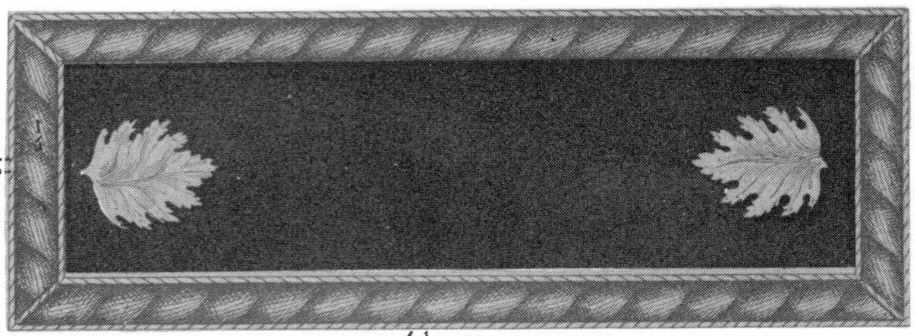

No. 287. 4¼ *Leaf in length 5/8. Stalk of leaf from end of Strap 3/8.*

PASSED ASSIST T SURGEONS.

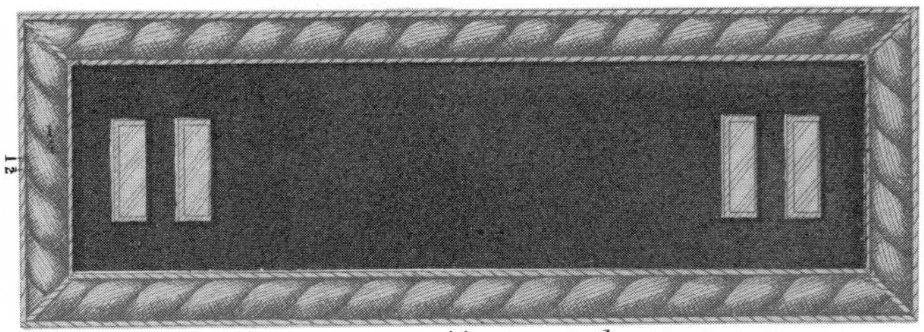

No. 288. 4¼ *Bars 2/10ths wide, 1/2 in. long. " 4/10ths from end of Strap. Space between bars 1/10th.*

ASSISTANT SURGEONS.

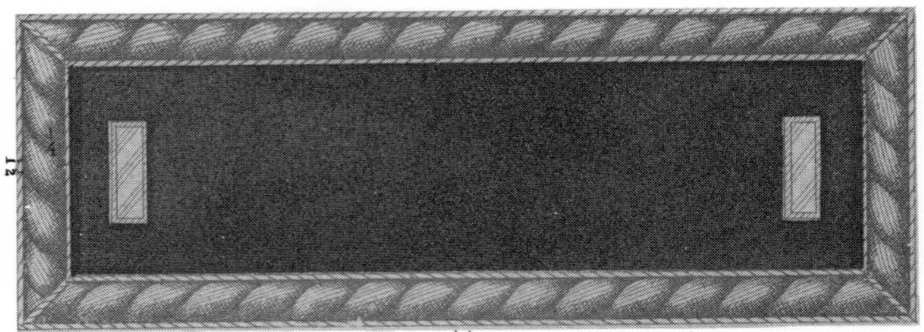

No. 289. 4¼ *Bar 2/10ths wide, 1/2 in. long. " 4/10ths from end of Strap.*

CHAPLAINS OF MORE THAN 12 YEARS.

No. 290. 4¼

CHAPLAINS OF LESS THAN 12 YEARS.

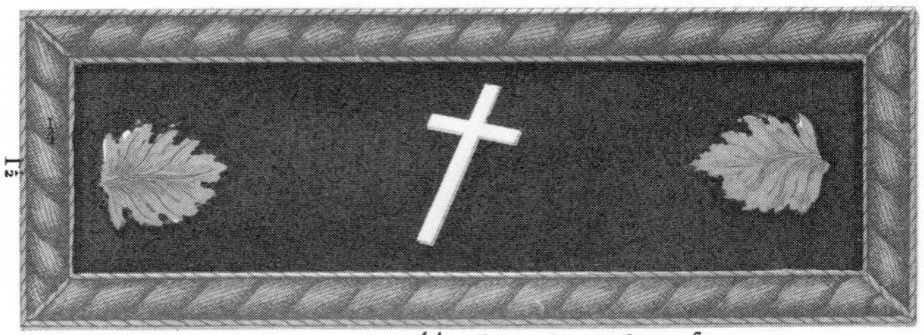

No. 291. 4¼ *Length of Cross 7/8. " of Leaf 5/8ths. Stalk of Leaf from end Strap 3/8.*

CHIEF OF BUREAU OF STEAM ENGINEERING.

No. 292. $4\frac{1}{4}$ *Center Ornament 1 in. long. Star in diam.r $\frac{7}{8}$ ths. Border $\frac{1}{4}$ in.*

FLEET ENGINEERS & CHIEF ENGINEERS AFTER 15 YEARS.

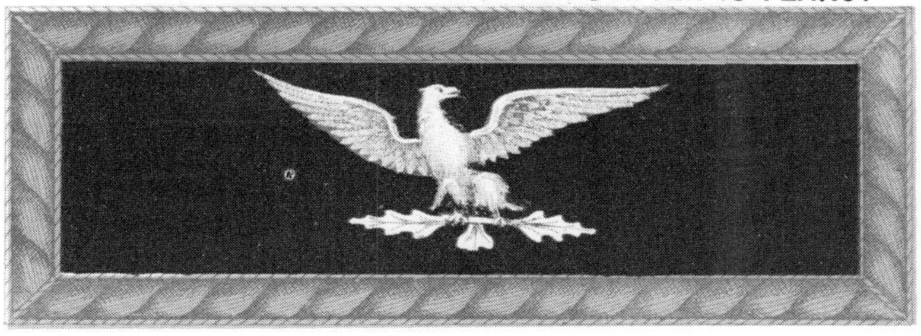

No. 293. *Eagle 2 in. from tip to tip. Spread of leaves $1\frac{1}{4}$ in.*

CHIEF ENGINEERS AFTER 1ST FIVE YEARS.

No. 294. *Leaf in length $\frac{5}{8}$. Stalk of leaf from end of Strap $\frac{3}{8}$.*

CHIEF ENGINEERS 1ST FIVE YEARS.

No. 295. *Leaf in length $\frac{5}{8}$. Stalk of leaf from end of Strap $\frac{3}{8}$.*

1ST ASSIST ENGINEERS.

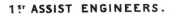

No. 296. *Bar $\frac{2}{10}$ ths wide, $\frac{1}{8}$ in. long. $\frac{4}{10}$ ths from end of Strap.*

2D ASSIST ENGINEERS.

No. 297. *Center Ornament 1 in. long.*

PROFESSORS OF LESS THAN 12 YEARS.

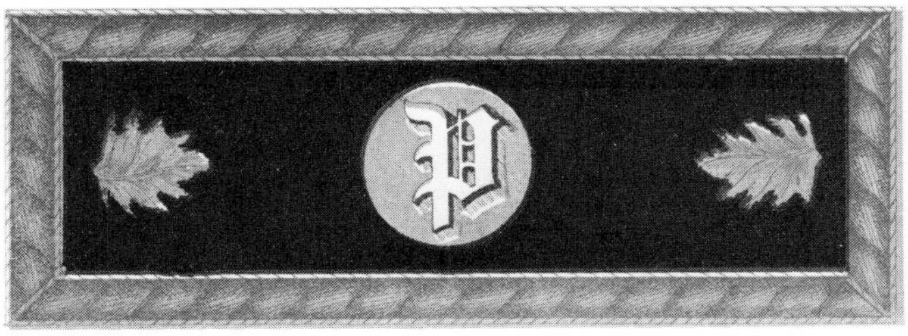

No. 298. *Plain center circle $\frac{5}{8}$ ths in. diam.r with letter in relief.*

PROFESSOR OVER 12 YEARS.— *same but Silver in place of Gold Emb.d Leaves.*

SECRETARIES.

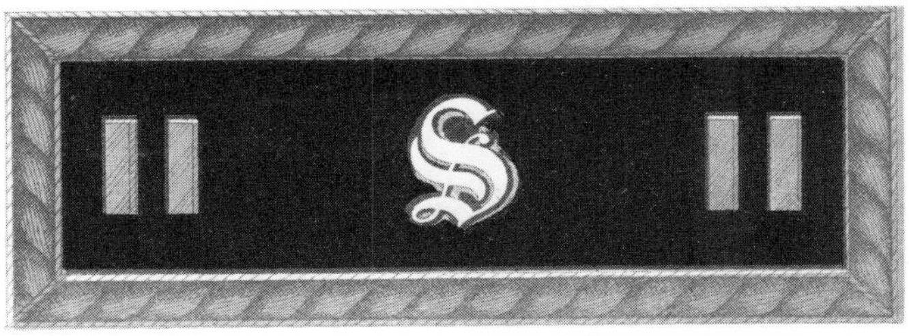

No. 299. *Bars $\frac{2}{10}$ ths wide, $\frac{1}{2}$ in. long. $\frac{4}{10}$ " from end of Strap. Space between bars $\frac{1}{10}$ th.*

No. 303. COMMANDER.

No. 307. ENSIGN.

No. 302. CAPTAIN.

No. 306. MASTER.

No. 301. COMMODORE.

No. 305. LIEUTENANT.

No. 300. REAR ADMIRAL.

No. 304. LIEUT. COMDR

Scale ¼ in. – 1 inch.

Note. Staff officers of assimilated rank to be the same
with the exeption of the Star.
Lace ¼ in, Spaces ¼ in. except where marked ½ inch.

U. S. Navy Shoulder Straps.

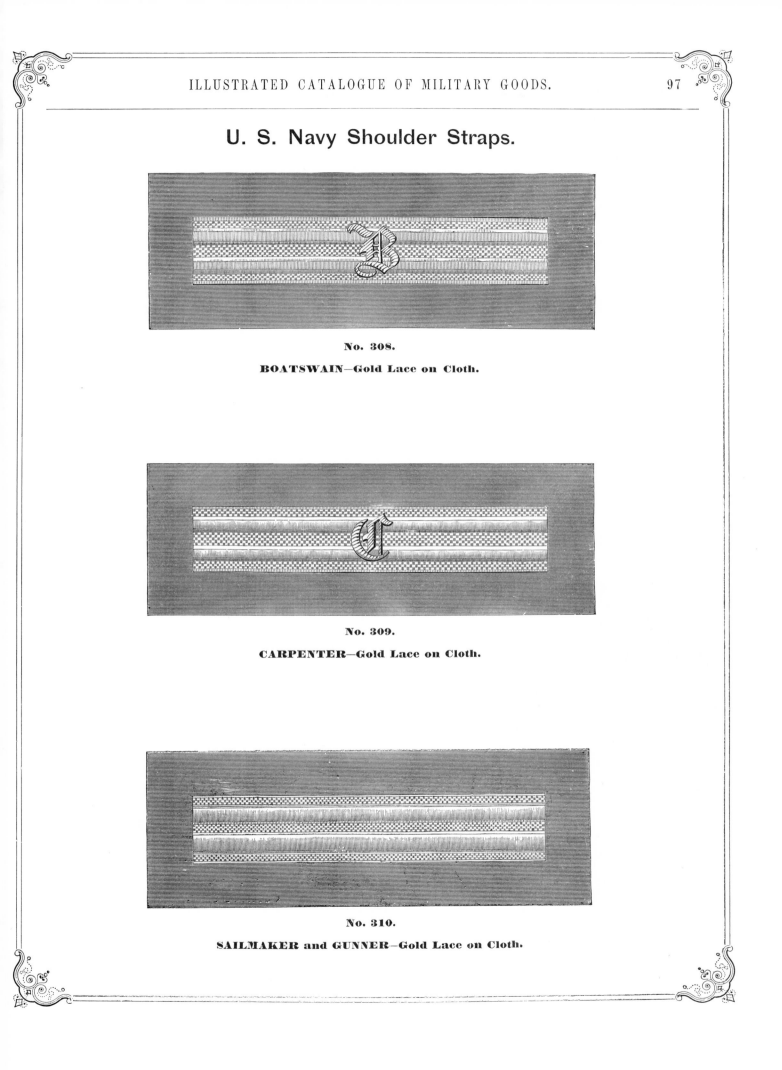

No. 308.

BOATSWAIN—Gold Lace on Cloth.

No. 309.

CARPENTER—Gold Lace on Cloth.

No. 310.

SAILMAKER and GUNNER—Gold Lace on Cloth.

Ornaments for Epaulettes designating Rank.

No. 311.
ADMIRAL.

Bullion, 3½ inches long, ⅝-inch diameter—
Devices in Silver.

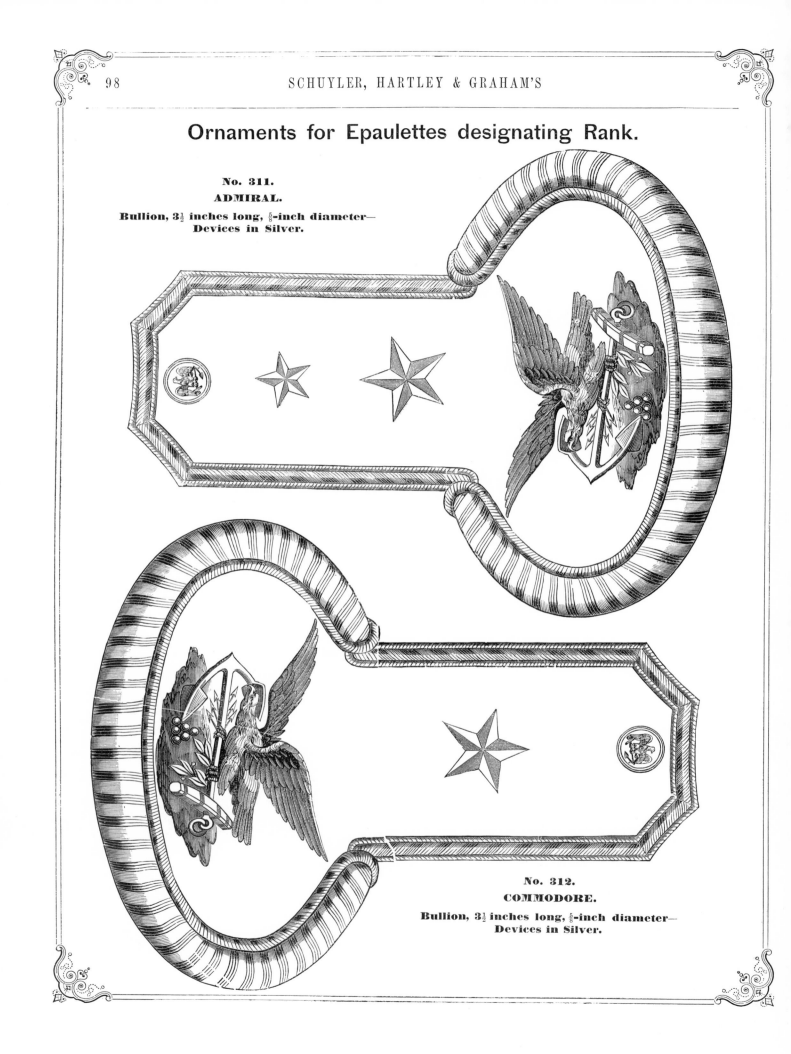

No. 312.

COMMODORE.

Bullion, 3½ inches long, ⅝-inch diameter—
Devices in Silver.

Ornaments for Epaulettes designating Rank.

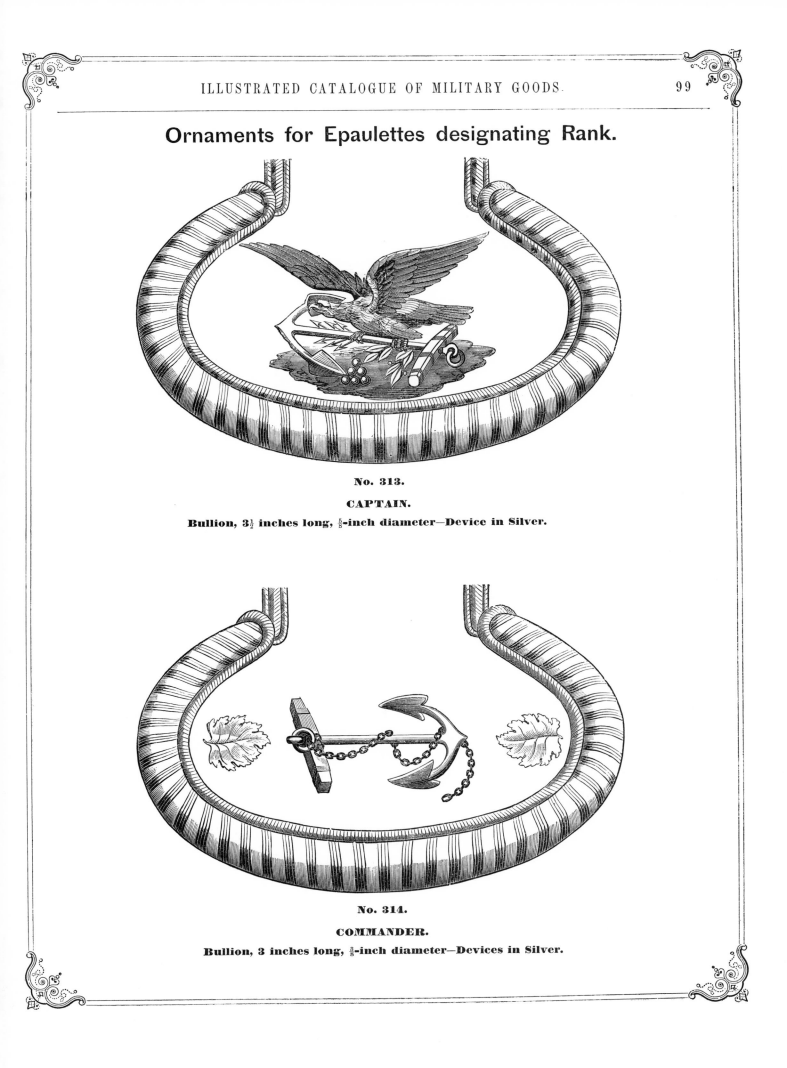

No. 313.

CAPTAIN.

Bullion, 3½ inches long, ⅝-inch diameter—Device in Silver.

No. 314.

COMMANDER.

Bullion, 3 inches long, ⅝-inch diameter—Devices in Silver.

Ornaments for Epaulettes designating Rank.

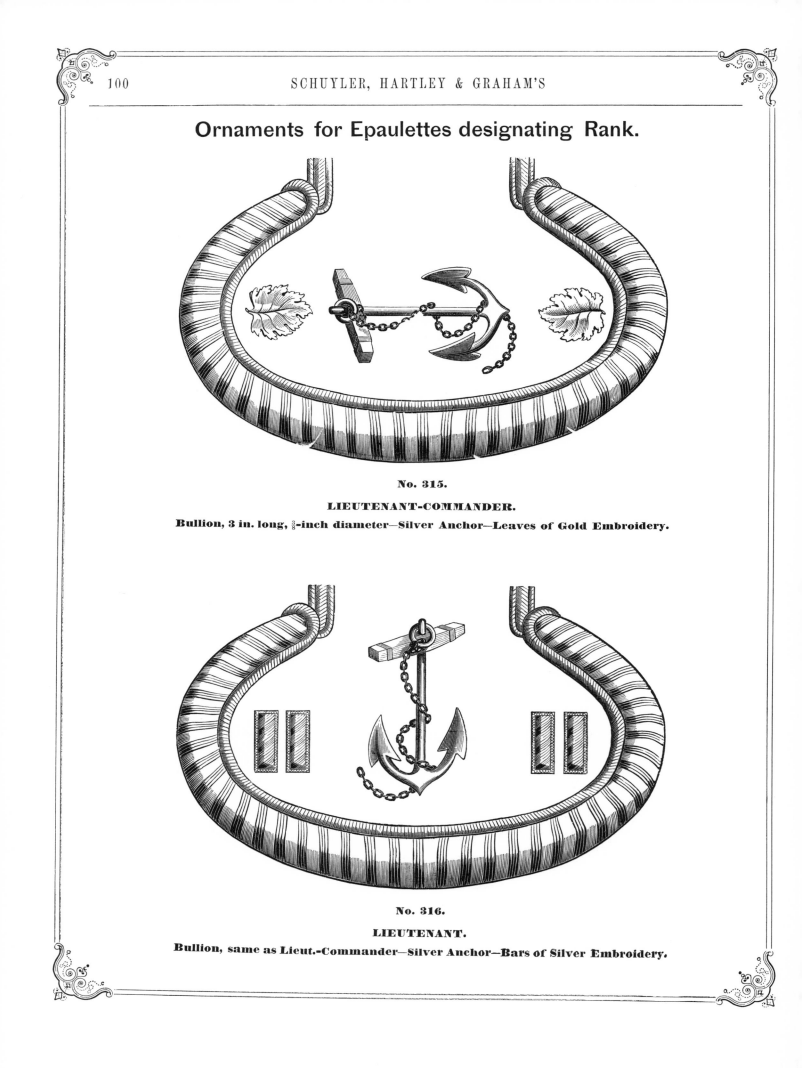

No. 315.

LIEUTENANT-COMMANDER.

Bullion, 3 in. long, ⅝-inch diameter—Silver Anchor—Leaves of Gold Embroidery.

No. 316.

LIEUTENANT.

Bullion, same as Lieut.-Commander—Silver Anchor—Bars of Silver Embroidery.

Ornaments for Epaulettes designating Rank.

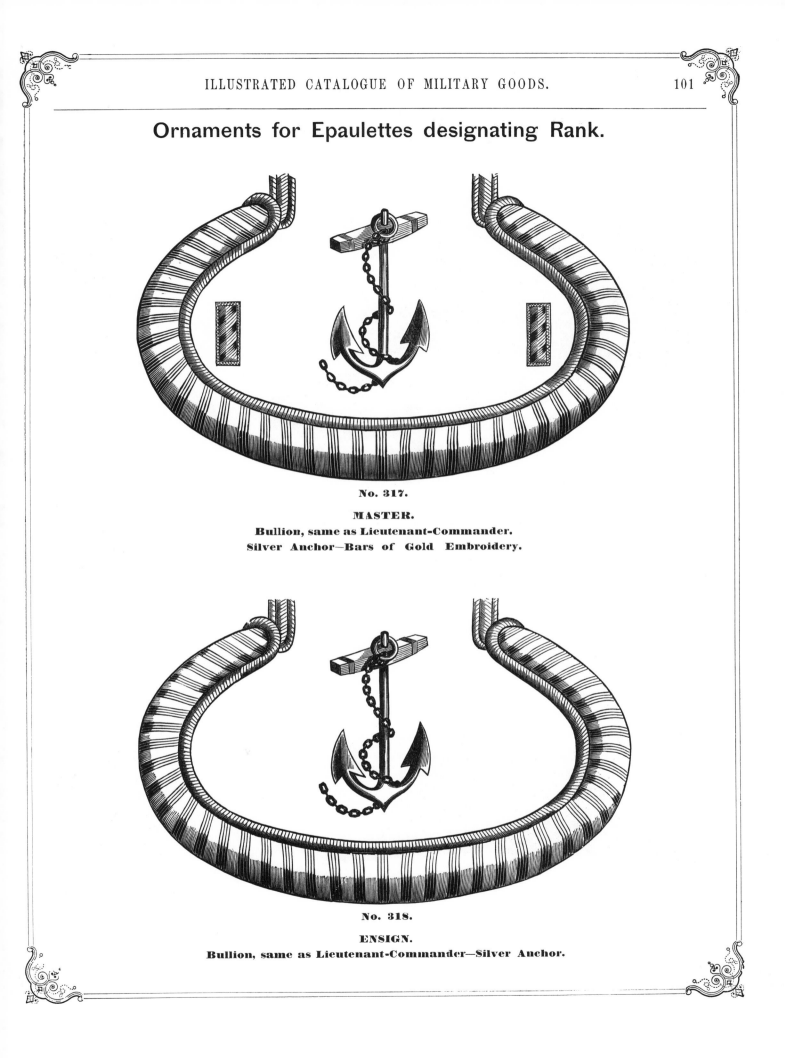

No. 317.

MASTER.

Bullion, same as Lieutenant-Commander.

Silver Anchor—Bars of Gold Embroidery.

No. 318.

ENSIGN.

Bullion, same as Lieutenant-Commander—Silver Anchor.

Navy Caps and Chapeaux.

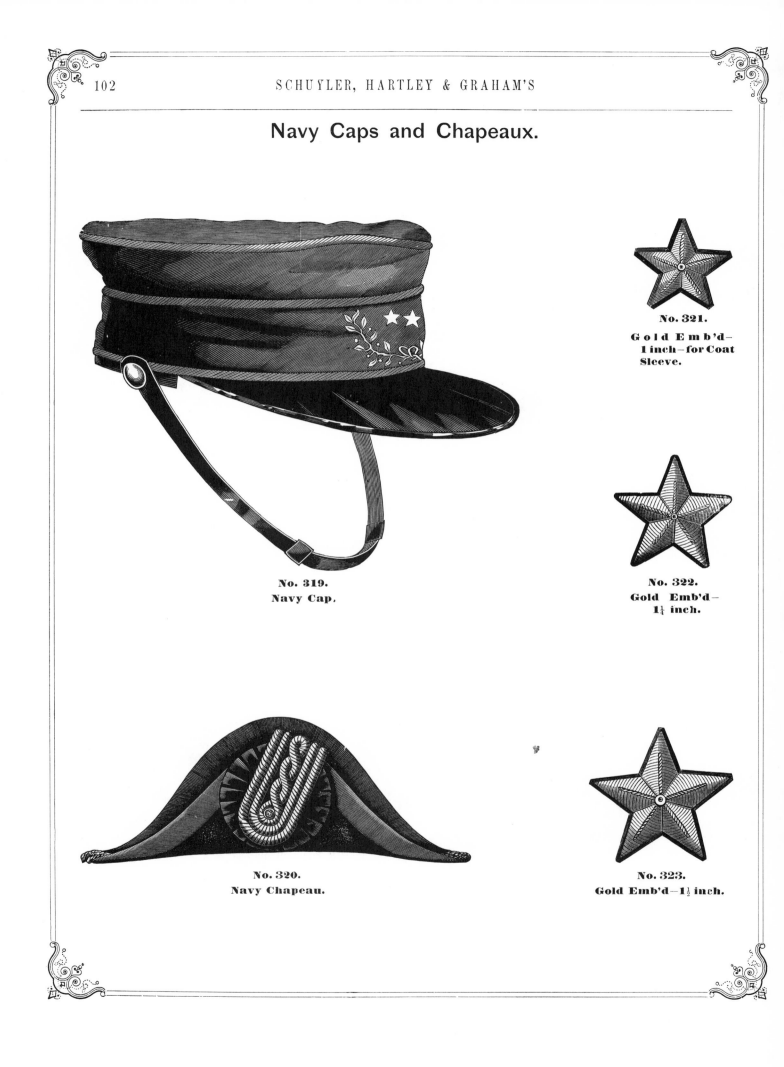

No. 319.
Navy Cap.

No. 320.
Navy Chapeau.

No. 321.
Gold Emb'd—
1 inch—for Coat
Sleeve.

No. 322.
Gold   Emb'd—
1¼ inch.

No. 323.
Gold Emb'd—1½ inch.

Lace and Belts.

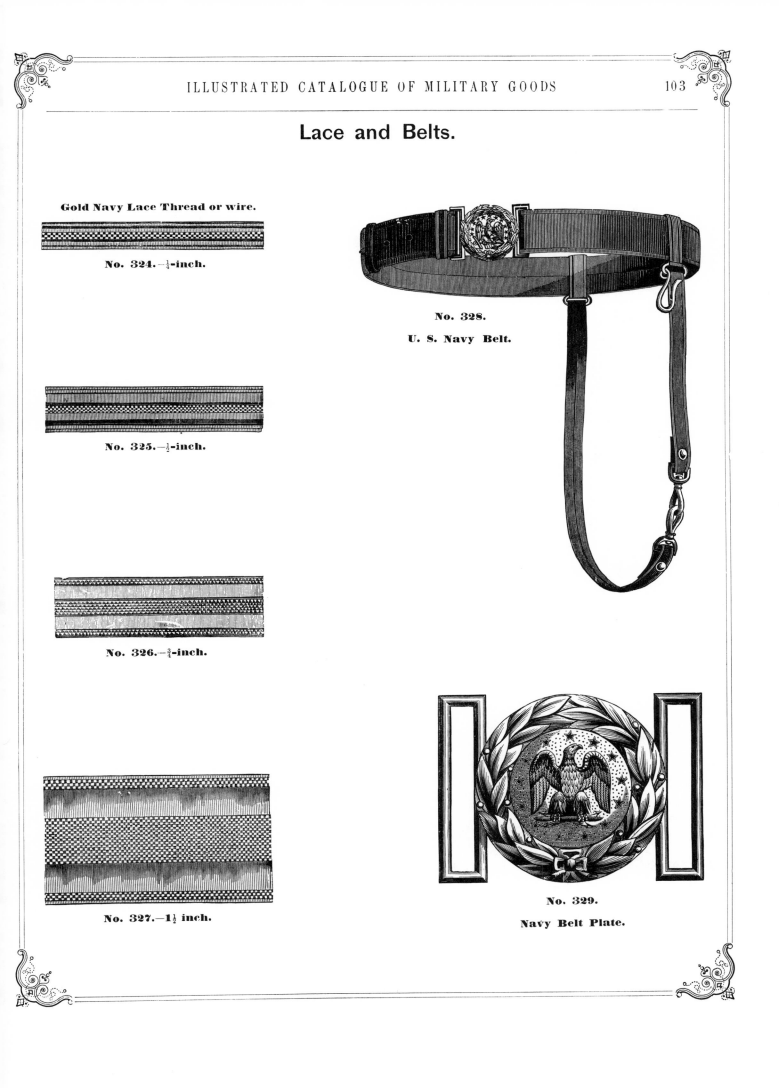

Gold Navy Lace Thread or wire.

No. 324.—¼-inch.

No. 325.—½-inch.

No. 326.—¾-inch.

No. 327.—1½ inch.

No. 328.

U. S. Navy Belt.

No. 329.

Navy Belt Plate.

MASONIC GOODS.

No. 330.
Gilt and Plated Tassels.

No. 331.
Gilt and Plated—1½ inch
to 5 inches.

No. 332.
Gilt and Plated.

No. 333.
Yellow and White Thread Fringes--
1 inch to 3 inch.

No. 334.
Gilt and Plated Bullion Fringes—
1 inch to 5 inches in width.

Masonic Goods.

No. 335.

Army Lace, ½-inch—Gold, Gilt, Silver, Plated, and Yellow.

No. 336.

U. S. Army, ½-inch—Gold, Silver, Gilt, Yellow, and Plated.

No. 337.

Thread Lace, ½-inch to 2¼-inch.

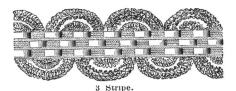

3 Stripe.

No. 338.

Limaeon Lace—1 Stripe—2 do.—3 do. —4 do.—5 do.

No. 339.

Braided Cord—Gilt, Gold, and Plated.

No. 340.

Vellum Lace, ¼-inch—Gold, Silver, Gilt, Plated, Yellow, and White.

No. 341.

Tinsel, or Lama Lace, ¼-inch to 2 inches—Yellow and White.

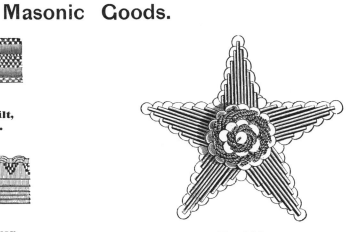

No. 342.

Gilt and Plated.
¾-inch to 1½-inch—Flat Centre.
1½-inch to 3½-inch—Raised Centre.

No. 343.

Gilt and Plated.
¾-inch to 1½-inch—Flat Centre.
1½-inch to 3½-inch—Raised Centre.

No. 344.

Grenade—Gilt and Gold.

REGULATIONS

FOR THE

OF THE

MARINE CORPS

UNIFORM AND DRESS

OF THE

𝔘𝔫𝔦𝔱𝔢𝔡 𝔖𝔱𝔞𝔱𝔢𝔰 𝔐𝔞𝔯𝔦𝔫𝔢 𝔠𝔬𝔯𝔭𝔰.

◄—••►

FULL DRESS.

COAT.

272. *Officers.*—All officers shall wear, in full dress, a double-breasted frock coat, of dark blue cloth, the skirt to extend three-fourths of the distance from the top of the hip to the bend of the knee.

273. *For the Commandant.*—Two rows of large size Marine buttons on the breast, eight in each row, placed in pairs; the distance between each row, five and one-half inches at top, and three and one-half inches at bottom; standing collar, to rise no higher than to permit the chin to turn freely over it; to hook in front at the bottom, and slope thence up and backward, at an angle of thirty degrees on each side, making the total opening in front an angle of sixty degrees; two loops of half-inch gold lace on each side of the collar, with one small Marine button at the end of each loop; the bottom loop four and one-half inches long, the upper loop not to extend further back than the bottom loop, and the front of both loops to slope up and backward with the front of the collar, at an angle of thirty degrees; collar to be edged all around with a scarlet edging; plain round cuff, three inches deep; slash on the sleeve, six and one-half inches long, and two and one-quarter inches wide at the points, and one and nine-tenths of an inch at the narrowest part of the curve; four loops of half-inch gold lace, and four small Marine buttons, one in each loop, on the slash of the sleeve; the loops on the sleeve to be two inches long, and one and one-eighth of an inch wide. The slash on the sleeve to be edged with scarlet on the ends and indented edges; pockets, with three-pointed side edges in the folds of the skirt; one button at the hip, one at the centre of the pocket opening, and one at the bottom, making six buttons on the back and skirt of the coat; the side edges to have one point on the centre of the edge, and to curve thence up and down to the top and bottom, corresponding with the slash on the sleeves; the side edges to be edged with scarlet on the ends and indented edges; lining of the coat, black.

274. *For Field Officers.*—Same as for the Commandant, except that there shall be eight buttons in each row, placed at equal distances.

275. *For Captains.*—Same as for field officers, except that there shall be but three loops of gold lace, and three small Marine buttons on the sleeve, and the slash shortened to correspond with the reduction in the number of loops.

276. *For Lieutenants.*—Same as for Captains, except that there shall be but two loops and small Marine buttons on the sleeve, and the slash shortened to correspond with the reduction in the number of loops

FOR ENLISTED MEN.

277. *For Sergeant-Major, Quartermaster-Sergeant, Drum-Major and Chief Musicians.*—Two rows of large size Marine buttons on the breast, seven in each row, placed at equal distances; the distance between each row, five and one-half inches at top, and three and one-half inches at bottom; standing collar, to rise no higher than to permit the chin to turn freely over it; to hook in front at the bottom, and slope thence up and backward at an angle of thirty degrees on each side, making the total opening in front an angle of sixty degrees; two loops of yellow worsted half-inch lace on each side of the collar, with one small Marine button at the end of each loop; the bottom loop four and one-half inches long; the upper loop not to extend further back than the bottom loop, and the front of both loops to slope up and backwards, with the front of the collar, at an angle of thirty degrees; collar to be edged all around with a scarlet edging, except those of the Drum-Major, Chief Musicians, and Musicians, which will be edged all around with white; plain round cuff, three inches deep; slash on the sleeve to be six inches long, and two and one-quarter inches wide at the points, and one and nine-tenths of an inch at the narrowest part of the curve; three loops of yellow worsted half-inch lace, and three small Marine buttons, one in the centre of each loop, on the slash of the sleeve; loops on the sleeve two inches long, and one inch and one-eighth wide; the slashed flap on the sleeve to be edged with scarlet on the ends and indented edges; those of the Drum-Major, Chief Musicians, and Musicians, to be edged with white; pockets with three-pointed edges in the fold of the skirt, one button at the hip, one at the centre of the pocket opening, and one at the bottom, making six buttons on the back and skirt of the coat; the pocket side edges to have one point at the centre of the edge, and to curve thence up and down to the top and bottom, corresponding with slash on the sleeve; the pocket side edges to be edged with scarlet on the ends and indented edges; those of the Drum-Major, Chief Musicians, and Musicians, to be edged with white. Lining of the coat, black. Skirts, full.

278. *For Sergeants.*—Same as for Sergeant-Major, except that there shall be but two loops, and two small Marine buttons on the slash of the sleeve, and that the slash shall be shortened to correspond with the reduction of the number of loops.

279. *For Corporals.*—Same as for Sergeants.

280. *For Privates.*—Same as for Corporals.

281. The uniform of all enlisted men, except the Drum-Major, Chief Musicians, and Musicians, shall be a double-breasted frock coat, of dark indigo blue cloth, with skirt extending three fourths of the distance from the top of the hip to the bend of the knee. Skirts, full.

282. *For Drum-Major, Chief Musicians, and Musicians.*—A scarlet, *cochineal* dyed, cloth, double-

breasted frock coat, with skirt extending three-fourths of the distance from the top of the hip to the bend of the knee.

283. *For Musicians.*—Same as for Privates, except that the coat shall be of *scarlet, cochineal* dyed, cloth, and the collar slashes on the sleeves, and the pocket side edges on the skirt, shall be edged with white, skirts, full.

CHEVRONS.

Shall be worn on the uniform coat, above the elbow, points up, of yellow silk lace, one-half inch wide, as follows:

284. *For a Sergeant-Major.*—Three bars and an arc, on a scarlet ground.

285. *For a Quartermaster-Sergeant.*—Three bars and a tie, on a scarlet ground.

286. *For a Drum-Major.*—Three bars and a tie, with a star in the centre, on a scarlet ground.

287. *For Sergeants.*—Chevrons of Yellow worsted half-inch lace, placed above the elbow, points up, as follows: For First Sergeants, three bars and a lozenge, edged with scarlet; other Sergeants, three bars, edged with scarlet.

288. *For a Corporal.*—Same as for Sergeants, except that the chevrons shall consist of two bars each.

BUTTONS.

289. Same as now worn.

TROWSERS.

290. The uniform trowsers, for both officers and enlisted men, shall, in cold weather, be of cloth, with French pockets, made loose, and to spread well over the boot, of white and light blue mixed, commonly called sky-blue mixture.

291. Officers *not* serving in line with troops, may wear dark blue cloth trowsers, with a welt of scarlet cloth let into each outer seam.

292. In warm weather, the uniform trowsers for both officers and enlisted men shall be of white linen. Both the cloth and linen trowsers shall be cut for enlisted men as shown in plates.

293. The cloth for the trowsers of enlisted men shall be of kersey.

294. Cloth trowsers for Commissioned Officers shall have a welt of scarlet, three-sixteenths of an inch in diameter, let into the outer seam.

295. For Sergeant-Major, Quartermaster-Sergeant, Drum-Major, Chief Musicians, and Musicians, a scarlet cord, three-sixteenths of an inch in diameter, down the outer seam.

CHAPEAU.

296. The Commandant and Field Officers shall wear a chapeau (French pattern) of the following dimensions: Length from point to point, from seventeen to nineteen inches; height of front, or cock, four and three-quarter inches; back or fan, five and one-half inches; points, two and five-eighths inches wide; to be bound with black lace (silk), to show five-eighths of an inch; at each end a gold and scarlet flat tassel, of fine gold and fine scarlet silk bullion; on the front, or cock, a black uncut velvet cockade, three inches in diameter; a loop of gold, one-half inch Marine lace, with a Marine coat-button at bottom of the loop; distance between the two strips of lace forming the loop, one quarter of an inch.

PLUME.

297. *For the Commandant.*—Of yellow swan feathers, bunched; length, twelve inches, drooping from a three-inch stem. Plume to be worn in a leather socket, placed inside of front or cock, four inches in advance of the gold loop.

298. *For Field Officers.*—Same as for Commandant, except that it shall be of cock or vulture feathers, and that the color shall be red.

UNIFORM CAP.

299. *Company Officers.*—Of fine black cloth; top, visor, and bands of fine glazed black leather; visor bound around the edges with the same; base line of cap to be *perfectly straight*, visor straight, and placed upon a continuation line; height of cap in front, from the rim under the visor, five and one-half inches; height of back six and one-half inches; difference of height between front and back, one inch; diameter of top, five and three-eighths inches; counter-sinking of top, three-eighths of an inch; width of lower black glazed leather band, one inch and one-eighth; width of upper black glazed leather band, seven-eighths of an inch; width of visor, six and three-quarter inches; depth, one inch and one-half.

300. *Enlisted Men.*—Same as for Company Officers, substituting black felt for cloth. For Drum-Major, of Astracan lambskin.

ORNAMENT.

301. *Company Officers.*—A United States Shield within a half wreath; resting upon the centre of the shield, a bugle and the letter M; the letter to be placed within the ring of the bugle, and to just fit that ring; the letter to be of *solid white metal, fastened on to the shield*; the shield, bugle and wreath to be of *yellow metal, heavily gilt.*

302. *Enlisted Men.*—Same as for Company Officers, except that the shield, bugle, and half wreath will not be gilt, but kept bright. The letter M will be of *white metal, like that on the ornament of the officer's cap.*

POMPON.

303. *For all Company Officers.*—Of gold net, two inches in height, and one and one-half inches in diameter, to be made over a cork foundation, of elliptical form; the pompon to be fixed to a wire loop, three inches long, and, when attached to the cap, to pitch forward in a line parallel with the rear slope of the cap; between the top of the shield in the ornament and the base of the pompon, a hemisphere of yellow metal, heavily gilt.

304. *For Enlisted Men, except the Drum-Major.*—A red worsted ball, five inches in circumference; when attached to the cap, to pitch forward in a line parallel with the rear of the slope of the cap. Between the top of the shield, in the ornament, and the base of the pompon, a hemisphere of yellow metal, to be kept bright, with a red leather ground just under the knot, above the shield on the uniform cap, extending out and scolloped, or cut in points so as to give effect.

305. *For the Drum-Major.*—Same as for enlisted men, except it shall be ten inches in circumference, to be fixed on a ring, the ring on a loop.

306. The uniform cap ornament, and pompon, will not be issued to enlisted men as part of the cap and clothing allowance, but will be served out *on charge*, to be returned at the expiration of each enlistment, and to be receipted for by an officer, as are arms and accoutrements.

STOCK.

307. *Officers.*—For all officers, black; when in uniform, the shirt collar will not appear more than one-fourth of an inch above the stock.

308. *For Enlisted Men.*—Of soft black leather, according to pattern in Quartermaster's Department.

BOOTS.

309. *Officers.*—Ankle or Jefferson.

310. *Enlisted Men.*—Of the pattern now furnished to the Infantry of the U. S. Army; to be made rights and lefts, and inspected before they are dressed off; the dressing to be done under the supervision of the Quartermaster's Department.

SPURS.

311. *For all Mounted Officers.*—Of yellow metal, or gilt.

GLOVES.

312. White.

SASH.

313. *For the Commandant.*—Of buff silk net, with silk bullion fringe ends; sash to go twice around

the waist, and to tie behind the left hip; pendant part not to extend more than eighteen inches below the tie.

314. *For Field and Company Officers.*—Of crimson silk net, to go around the waist, and tie, as for the Commandant. The Sash will be worn by "Officers of the day" across the body, scarf fashion, from the right shoulder to the left side, instead of around the waist, tying behind the left hip.

315. *For Sergeant-Major, Quartermaster-Sergeant, Drum-Major, Chief Musicians, and First Sergeants.*—Of red worsted, with worsted bullion fringe ends, to go twice around the waist, and to tie behind the left hip; pendant part not to extend more than eighteen inches below the tie. The sash will be worn (over the coat) on all occasions of duty of every description, except fatigue.

SWORD BELT.

316. *For all Officers.*—A waist belt not less than one and one-half inches, nor more than two inches wide to be worn over the sash; the sword to be suspended from it by slings of the same material as the belt, with a hook attached to the belt, upon which the sword may be hung.

317. *For the Commandant.*—Of Russia leather, with three stripes of gold embroidery; the slings embroidered on both sides; or the same belt as to be immediately prescribed for all other officers.

318. *For all other officers.*—Of white glazed leather.

SWORD BELT PLATE.

319. *For all Officers.*—Gilt rectangular, two inches wide, with a raised bright rim; a wreath of laurel encircling the Arms of the "United States:" eagle, shield, scroll, edge of cloud, and rays, bright.

SWORD AND SCABBARD.

320. *For the Commandant.*—Either a sword of honor, presented by the General Government, or that of a State, or the sword prescribed for all other officers.

321. *All other Officers.*—The sword of the pattern adopted by the War Department, April 9th, 1850.

322. *For Enlisted Men.*—Same as U. S. Infantry.

SWORD KNOT.

323. *For all Officers.*—Gold lace strap, with gold bullion tassel.

EPAULETTES.

324. *For the Commandant.*—Gold, with solid crescent; device of the Corps; a bugle of solid silver

containing the letter M within the ring of the bugle; bugle and letter same size as that worn on the undress cap. This device to be placed within the crescent; on the centre of the strap, a silver embroidered star one and one-eighth inches in diameter, dead and bright bullion one-half inch in diameter, and three and one-half inches long.

325. *For a Colonel.*—Same as for the Commandant, substituting a silver embroidered spread-eagle for the star upon the strap.

326. *For a Lieutenant-Colonel.*—Same as for the Commandant, substituting for the star, a silver embroidered leaf upon the strap.

327. *For a Major.*—Same as for the Commandant, *without the star on the centre of the strap.*

328. *For a Captain.*—Same as for the Commandant, except that the bullion will be only one-fourth of an inch in diameter, and two and one-half inches long; and substituting for the star two silver embroidered bars.

229. *For a First-Lieutenant.*—Same as for the Commandant, except that the bullion will be only one-eighth of an inch in diameter, and two and one-half inches long; and substituting for the star one embroidered silver bar.

330. *For a Second-Lieutenant.*—Same as for a First Lieutenant, omitting the silver embroidered bar.

331. Epaulettes will only be worn in full dress.

332. Full dress shall be worn on parades, occasions of ceremony, and on Marine General Courts-Martial.

333. *For Enlisted Men.*—Yellow metal crescent, and scale strap, with yellow worsted bullion; the bullion to be removable, in order to clean the metal.

334. *For Sergeant-Major, Quartermaster-Sergeant, Drum-Major, and Chief Musicians.*—Bullion three and one-half inches long, and three-eighths of an inch in diameter.

335. *For Sergeants.*—Same as for Sergeant-Major, except the bullion will be only one quarter of an inch in diameter.

336. *For Corporals.*—Same as for Sergeant-Major, except that the bullion will be only one-sixteenth of an inch in diameter.

337. *For Privates.*—Same as for Corporals.

338. The metallic crescent and scale strap will be made according to pattern.

339. The metallic crescent and scale strap will not be issued as part of the clothing allowance, but will be served out *on charge;* to be returned at the expiration of each enlistment, and to be receipted for by an officer, as are arms and accoutrements.

UNDRESS COAT.

340. *Officers.*—For all officers, a double-breasted dark blue cloth frock coat, the skirt to extend three-fourths of the distance from the top of the hip to the bend of the knee. Skirts full.

341. *For the Commandant.*—Two rows of buttons on the breast, eight in each row, placed in pairs; the distance between each row, five and one-half inches at top, and three and one-half inches at bottom;

stand-up collar, to rise no higher than to permit the chin to turn freely over it; to hook at the bottom, in front, and slope thence up and backward at an angle of thirty degrees on each side, making the total opening in front an angle of sixty degrees; cuffs two and one-half inches deep, to go around the sleeve parallel with the lower edge, and to button with three small buttons at the under seam; pockets in the folds of the skirts, with one button at hip, and one at the end of each pocket, making four buttons on the back and skirt of the coat; collar and cuffs to be of dark blue velvet; lining of the coat black.

342. *For all other Officers.*—Same as the Commandant, except that the buttons on the breast will be placed at equal distances; collar aad cuffs of the same material and color as the coat.

343. *For Enlisted Men.*—A single-breasted dark indigo blue kersey frock coat; one row of seven Marine buttons on the breast; stand-up collar (with a red welt inserted in the seam, where the collar joins the coat), to rise no higher than to permit the chin to turn freely over it, to hook in front at bottom, and slope thence up and backward at an angle of thirty degrees on each side, making the whole opening in front an angle of sixty degrees; cuffs two and one half inches deep, to go around the sleeves parallel with the lower edge, and to button with two small Marine buttons; skirt of the coat to extend from the top of the hip to the crotch of the trowsers, with one button over the hip, making two buttons on the back of the coat; no pockets in the skirts; lining of the coat black. Skirts to be full. Non-commissioned Officers will wear chevrons of their grades (as prescribed in the full dress) above the elbow, points up.

FATIGUE SACKS.

344. All enlisted men on board of sea-going vessels will wear a flannel fatigue sack, of dark indigo blue; open half-way down the front, and buttoning with four small Marine buttons; yoke on the shoulder; the sack to extend in length half the distance from the top of the hip to the bend of the knee; small turn-down collar of the same material; sleeves like a coat sleeve, but without cuff or opening, and made larger at the wrist, to permit the free passage of the hand; seams at the side to be closed up all the way down. Non-commissioned Officers will wear the chevrons of their grade (as prescribed in the full dress) on the sleeves above the elbow, points up. No lining.

SUMMER FATIGUE COAT.

345. *Officers.*—On ship board, the Summer Coat for Officers shall be of white linen, made like the blue cloth undress coat. This coat may be worn, at their pleasure, by officers visiting the shore in foreign ports, except on occasions of parade or ceremony. When this coat is worn, the shoulder knot, to be hereinafter prescribed, shall also be worn.

346. The fatigue sack for enlisted men shall be worn at sea in warm weather; and in the tropics, on ordinary occasions, in port also. When worn, it must be with a white shirt underneath.

FATIGUE CAP.

347. *Officers.*—All officers shall wear, in undress, a dark blue cloth cap, according to pattern; black

ribbed silk band one inch and five-eighths of an inch wide; three rows of black silk braid, three-sixteenths of an inch wide down each seam from the crown to the bottom; in the centre of crown a knot of the same braid, and also one row around the edge of the crown; vizor six and one-half inches wide, and one and one-half inches deep.

348. *Enlisted Men.*—Same as officers, except the silk band and braid. The lining in the band and crown to be of prepared leather.

ORNAMENT.

349. *Officers.*—A Gold embroidered bugle, two and one-quarter inches long, and one and five-sixteenths greatest width; solid silver or plated M within the centre of the ring of the bugle, the letter to be made with an eye on the back, like a button, that it may be removed and cleaned; bugle to be embroidered on scarlet cloth, which will be trimmed off, so as to present a margin of one-eighth of an inch, following the line of the embroidery.

350. *For Enlisted Men.*—For all enlisted men, a bugle of yellow metal same size as that of the officer, the letter M in white metal; the letter to rest on a circular piece of red leather; both bugle and letter to be fastened with eyes and rings, on leather strips. The undress cap to be provided with a water-proof cover, according to pattern sent to Quartermaster's Department.

SHOULDER KNOT.

351. *Officers.*—All officers shall wear on each shoulder of the undress coat, and undress white linen coat, a shoulder knot of *fine gold cord* three-sixteenths of an inch in diameter, the shoulder knot to consist of a twisted strap, and an end of a clover leaf shape; the clover leaf end to be lined with scarlet cloth, to show through the openings; the twisted strap to be also lined, *only* so as to show through the *openings;* there will be no cushion under the end which rests on the shoulder and the twisted strap extending from thence up to the coat collar; the knot to be fastened by a small Marine button, and tags at the collar; and at the shoulder two tags; tags to pass through the cloth of the coat and tie on the inside.

352. *For the Commandant.*—Four cords in the twisted strap and clover leaf end, with a silver embroidered star in the centre of the clover leaf.

353. *For a Colonel.*—Same as for the commandant, substituting a silver embroidered spread eagle for the star.

354. *For a Lieutenant-Colonel.*—Same as for the Commandant, substituting a silver embroiderd leaf for the star.

355. *For a Major.*—Same as for the Commandant, but without any device.

356. *For Captains.*—Of three cords, with two silver embroidered bars in the clover leaf ends.

357. *For First Lieutenants.*—Same as for Captains, omitting one of the bars.

358. *For Second Lieutenants.*—Same as for Captains, but without any device.

OVERCOAT.

359. *Officers.*—A "cloak coat" of dark blue cloth, lined with scarlet woolen, and closing by means of our frog olive-shaped buttons, of black silk, one inch and one-eighth in length, and loops of black silk cord down the breast, and at the throat by a long loop *a echelle* without tassel or plate, on the left side, and a black silk frog button on the right; cord for the loops three-sixteenths of an inch in diameter; back a single piece, slit up from the bottom, from fifteen to seventeen inches, according to the height of the wearer, and closing at will, by buttons and button-holes in a fly-flap; collar of the same color and material as the coat, rounded at the edges, and to stand or fall; when standing, to be about five inches high; side pieces, with the pockets cut according to pattern. Sleeves loose, of a single piece, and round at the bottom without cuff or slit; the sleeves to be cut according to pattern. Around the front, the lower border, the edges of the pockets, the edges of the sleeves, collar and slit in the back, a flat braid of black silk, one-half an inch wide; and around each frog button on the breast, a knot two and one-quarter inches in diameter, of black silk cord, one-sixteenth of an inch in diameter. A cape of the same color and material as the coat, removable at the pleasure of the wearer, and reaching to the edge of the coat sleeve when the arm is extended; lining of cape black; coat to extend down the leg from six to eight inches below the knee, according to height. *To indicate rank*, there will be on both sleeves, near the lower edge, a knot of flat black silk braid, one-eighth of an inch in width, and composed as follows:

360. *For the Commandant.*—Of five braids, double knot.

361. *For a Colonel.*—Of five braids, single knot.

362. *For a Lieutenant-Colonel.*—Of four braids, single knot.

363. *For a Major.*—Of three braids, single knot.

364. *For a Captain.*—Of two braids, single knot.

365. *For a First Lieutenant.*—Of one braid, single knot.

366. *For a Second Lieutenant.*—A plain sleeve, without knot or ornament.

367. *Enlisted Men.*—Of blue gray mixture, stand-up collar; single breasted, with one row of seven large Marine buttons on the breast; loose sleeves, with cuffs five inches deep; cape to be cut circularly, and to reach down in front to the upper edge of the cuff when the arm is extended, and to button all the way down in front, with five small Marine buttons. The cape to be made separate from the coat, and to be buttoned on. Non-commissioned Officers shall wear the chevrons of their grade, as prescribed for the full dress coat, on the cuffs of their overcoats.

OTHER ARTICLES OF CLOTHING

368. *Officers.*—Officers may wear a fatigue jacket of dark blue cloth, lined with scarlet, collar same as undress coat, but edged all around with one-half inch gold lace; pointed cuff, point up, six inches deep, and edged all around with half-inch gold lace, sixteen small Marine buttons in a single row in front and at the opening of the sleeve; shoulder knots will be worn with the fatigue jacket.

369. *Enlisted Men.*—The flannel shirts shall be changed in color from *red* to *blue.*

370. The blankets to be *all wool,* and to weigh four pounds; color gray, with the letters U. S. M. in black, four inches long; blankets to be seven feet long, and five and a half feet wide; the letters U. S. M. to be placed in the centre.

371. Allowances of clothing for an enlistment of four years, as follows:

One uniform cap, two uniform coats, two sets of epaulette bullion, seven pairs linen trowsers, eight pairs of woolen trowsers, twelve shirts, two stocks, sixteen pairs of shoes, one blanket, eight pairs of socks, eight pairs of drawers, four fatigue caps, four fatigue coats, eight blue flannel shirts, one great coat.

372. After a guard marches on board of a sea-going vessel, each enlisted man shall be entitled to receive the additional articles of clothing following: one great coat (*on charge, and only to be worn, under direction of Commanding Marine Officer in port, when the men are posted, or formed as a guard of honor on the quarter-deck; at all other times to be kept in the Marine Store-room; these extra coats to be worn, on post, by day only, in clear, cold weather*), and two dark blue flannel sacks.

EQUIPMENTS.

BELTS.

373. All enlisted men shall wear white waist belts of the French pattern, with the French clasp and knapsack sliding slings; the cartridge box to be attached to the belt by a leather loop, and to slide by it along the belt, the bayonet scabbard to be attached to the belt by a frog, also sliding on the belt: Non-commissioned Officers wearing swords, as also Musicians, will wear their swords in a sliding frog.

374. *Drum Sling.*—White webbing, provided with a brass drum-stick carriage.

KNAPSACK.

375. Of cow-skin (*black*), and to be made and slung, *according to pattern in the Quartermaster's Department, Headquarters.*

HAVERSACK.

376. Of same material, size, and form, as those issued to the United States Army.

CANTEENS.

377. Same as used in United States Army.

MUSKET SLINGS.

378. The Musket Slings to be of black leather; muskets will not be put into the hands of troops without the slings.

379. The Knapsack, Haversack, Canteens, and Musket Slings, will be served out *on charge*, and receipted for by an officer, as are arms and other equipments. *Knapsacks, Haversacks, and Canteens* will be kept in the store-room on shipboard, and put in the hands of the troops when occasion requires.

REGULATIONS

FOR THE

Uniform and Dress

OF THE

U. S. REVENUE CUTTER SERVICE

Of the United States.

UNIFORM AND DRESS

OF THE

U. S. Revenue Cutter Service.

— • —

380. Revenue officers are required to provide themselves with the uniforms prescribed by the Regulations, to wear them on board the vessels to which they belong, and while on duty in boarding vessels, and elsewhere.

381. The uniform established to distinguish the officers of the revenue cutter service is as follows:

DECK OFFICERS.

382. *Captain's Full Dress.*—Blue cloth frock coat, with rolling collar, double-breasted, lined with black silk, nine buttons on each lappel, two on upper part of skirt, and two on lower part of skirt; two strips of half-inch gold lace around the upper part of each cuff; two plain gold epaulettes; blue cloth Navy cap, with one band of gold lace, with ornament of Treasury shield within wreath in gold; with navy regulation sword; black silk cravat or stock; buff, blue, or white vest (according to the season), single-breasted, with nine buttons in front; blue pantaloons, with stripe of gold lace on outer seam, or white pantaloons, according to season.

383. *Captain's Undress.*—Same as full dress, substituting for the epaulettes a shoulder strap on each shoulder, of blue cloth, with raised gold edging; in the centre, two cross foul anchors; all of them to be worked in gold.

384. *First Lieutenant's Full Dress.*—Same as captain, with the exception of one strip of lace on the cuff, and cap with one foul anchor, over shield, with wreath, all in gold.

385. *Undress.*—The same as captain, with the same exceptions; shoulder strap to be with one foul anchor over shield, and two bars at each end; cap the same as in full dress.

386. *Second Lieutenant.*—Dress and undress same as first lieutenant, omitting one bar at each end of shoulder strap.

387. *Third Lieutenant.*—Dress and undress same as second lieutenant, omitting bars on shoulder straps.

ENGINEERS.

388. *Chief Engineer's Dress and Undress.*—Same as first lieutenant. Shoulder strap blue cloth, with raised gold edging, with gold wheel, surmounted by anchor; cap with band, with wheel surmounted by star within wreath, all in gold.

389. *First Assistant Engineers.*—Same as chief engineer, substituting three buttons on cuff, in lieu of lace; shoulder strap same as chief engineer, omitting anchor; cap with gold band, with wheel inside of wreath, omitting star.

390. *Second Assistant.*—Same as first assistant, omitting wheel on strap and cap.

391. *Petty Officer's Dress.*—Blue cloth jacket, with nine revenue buttons on each lappel, three under each pocket flap, and three on each cuff; white or blue pantaloons (according to season).

392. Seamen, firemen, coal-passers, stewards, cooks, and boys, white frock, with collar and facings of blue, or blue frock (according to season); white or blue trousers; blue mustering cap or sennet hat.

ARMS AND AMMUNITION.

ARMS AND AMMUNITION.

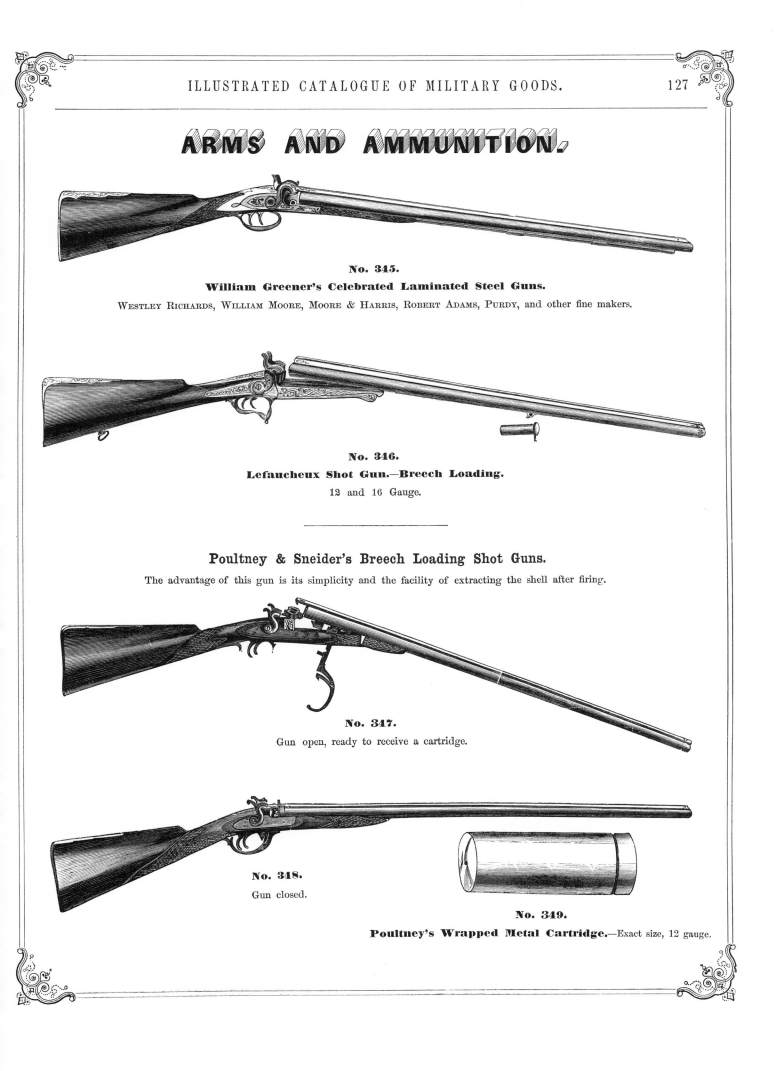

No. 345.

William Greener's Celebrated Laminated Steel Guns.

WESTLEY RICHARDS, WILLIAM MOORE, MOORE & HARRIS, ROBERT ADAMS, PURDY, and other fine makers.

No. 346.

Lefaucheux Shot Gun.—Breech Loading.

12 and 16 Gauge.

Poultney & Sneider's Breech Loading Shot Guns.

The advantage of this gun is its simplicity and the facility of extracting the shell after firing.

No. 347.

Gun open, ready to receive a cartridge.

No. 348.

Gun closed.

No. 349.

Poultney's Wrapped Metal Cartridge.—Exact size, 12 gauge.

Arms and Ammunition.

Sharp's Rifles and Shot Guns.

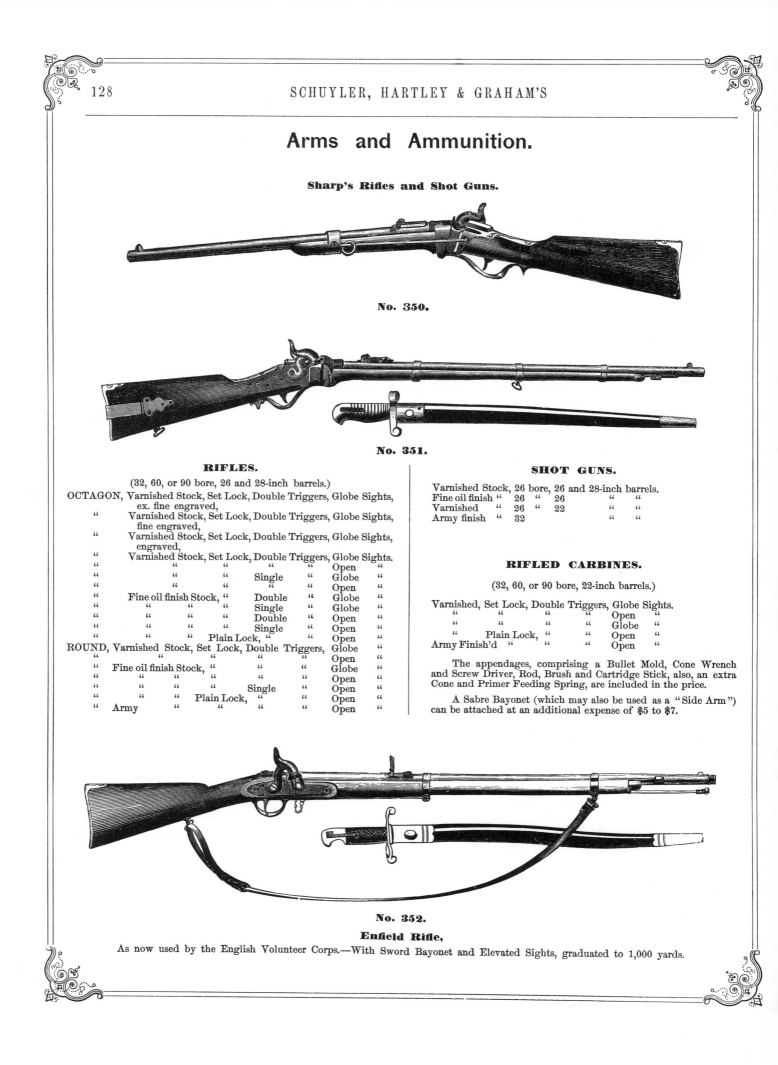

No. 350.

No. 351.

RIFLES.

(32, 60, or 90 bore, 26 and 28-inch barrels.)

OCTAGON,	Varnished Stock, Set Lock, Double Triggers, Globe Sights, ex. fine engraved,					
"	Varnished Stock, Set Lock, Double Triggers, Globe Sights, fine engraved,					
"	Varnished Stock, Set Lock, Double Triggers, Globe Sights, engraved,					
"	Varnished Stock, Set Lock, Double Triggers, Globe Sights.					
"	"	"	"	"	Open	"
"	"	"	Single	"	Globe	"
"	"	"	"	"	Open	"
"	Fine oil finish Stock,	"	Double	"	Globe	"
"	"	"	"	Single	"	Globe	"
"	"	"	"	Double	"	Open	"
"	"	"	"	Single	"	Open	"
"	"	"	Plain Lock,	"	"	Open	"
ROUND,	Varnished Stock, Set Lock, Double Triggers,		Globe	"
"	"	"	"	"	Open	"
"	Fine oil finish Stock,	"	"	"	Globe	"
"	"	"	"	"	Open	"
"	"	"	"	"	Open	"
"	"	"	"	Single	"	Open	"
"	"	"	Plain Lock,	"	"	Open	"
"	Army	"	"	"	"	Open	"

SHOT GUNS.

Varnished Stock,	26 bore,	26 and 28-inch barrels.			
Fine oil finish "	26 "	26	"	"	
Varnished "	26 "	22	"	"	
Army finish "	32				

RIFLED CARBINES.

(32, 60, or 90 bore, 22-inch barrels.)

Varnished, Set Lock, Double Triggers, Globe Sights.					
"	"	"	"	Open	"
"	"	"	"	Globe	"
"	Plain Lock,	"	"	Open	"
Army Finish'd	"	"	"	Open	"

The appendages, comprising a Bullet Mold, Cone Wrench and Screw Driver, Rod, Brush and Cartridge Stick, also, an extra Cone and Primer Feeding Spring, are included in the price.

A Sabre Bayonet (which may also be used as a "Side Arm") can be attached at an additional expense of $5 to $7.

No. 352.

Enfield Rifle,

As now used by the English Volunteer Corps.—With Sword Bayonet and Elevated Sights, graduated to 1,000 yards.

Arms and Ammunition.

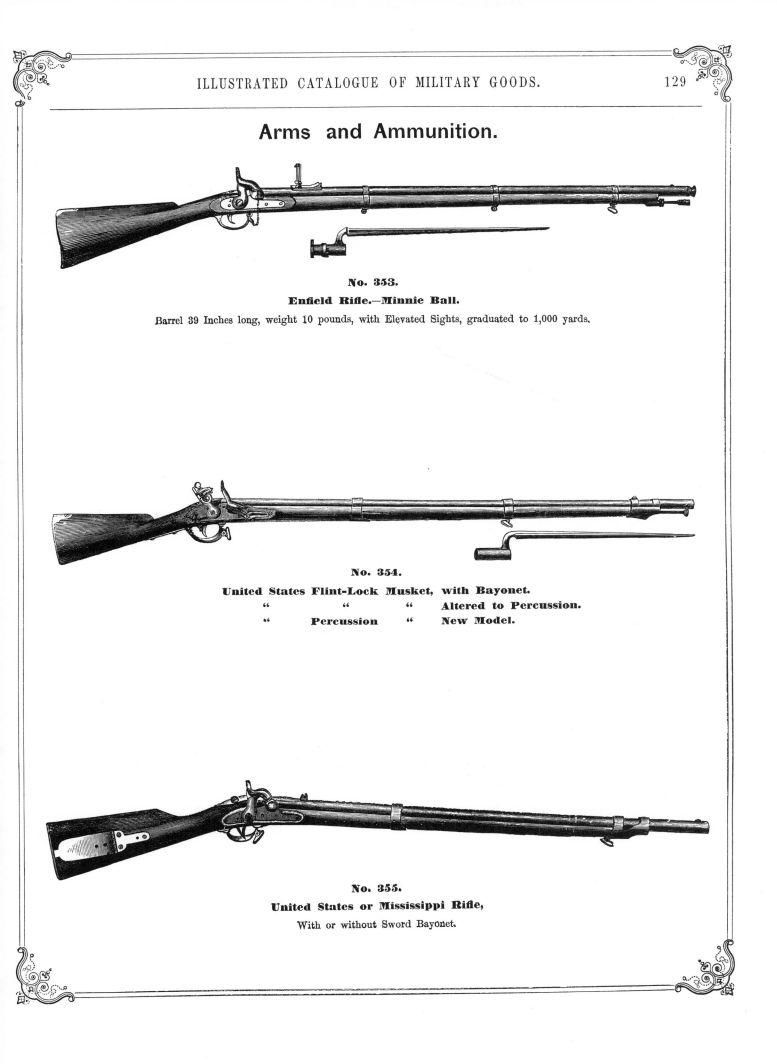

No. 353.

Enfield Rifle.—Minnie Ball.

Barrel 39 Inches long, weight 10 pounds, with Elevated Sights, graduated to 1,000 yards.

No. 354.

United States Flint-Lock Musket, with Bayonet.
      "   "   "   Altered to Percussion.
      "   Percussion   "   New Model.

No. 355.

United States or Mississippi Rifle,

With or without Sword Bayonet.

Arms and Ammunition.

Burnside's Patent Breech Loading Carbines.

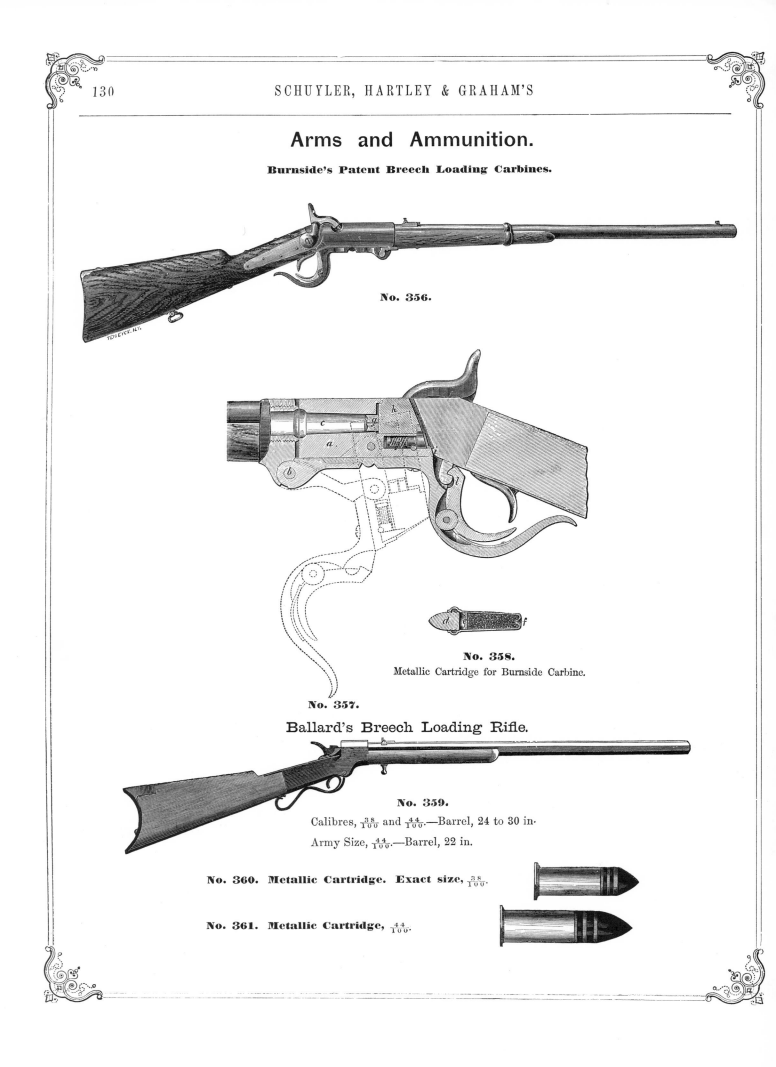

No. 356.

No. 358.

Metallic Cartridge for Burnside Carbine.

No. 357.

Ballard's Breech Loading Rifle.

No. 359.

Calibres, $\frac{38}{100}$ and $\frac{44}{100}$.—Barrel, 24 to 30 in.

Army Size, $\frac{44}{100}$.—Barrel, 22 in.

No. 360. Metallic Cartridge. Exact size, $\frac{38}{100}$.

No. 361. Metallic Cartridge, $\frac{44}{100}$.

Arms and Ammunition.

Joslyn Carbine.

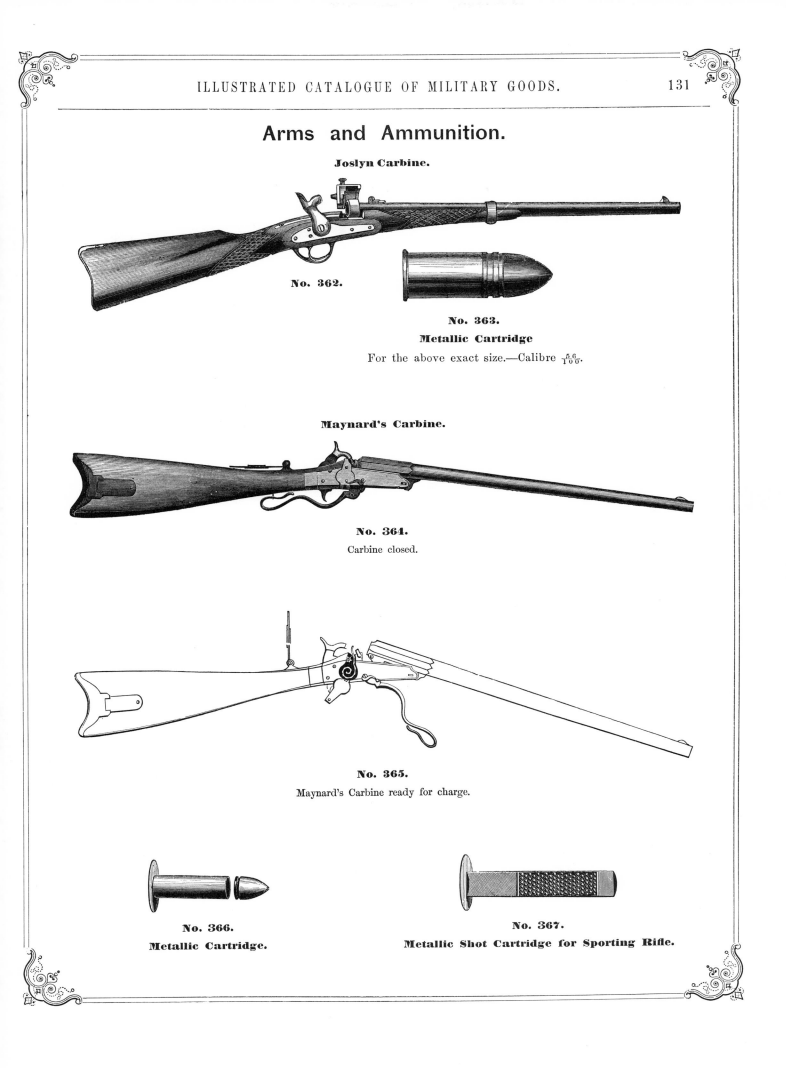

No. 362.

No. 363.

Metallic Cartridge

For the above exact size.—Calibre $\frac{56}{100}$.

Maynard's Carbine.

No. 364.

Carbine closed.

No. 365.

Maynard's Carbine ready for charge.

No. 366.

Metallic Cartridge.

No. 367.

Metallic Shot Cartridge for Sporting Rifle.

Arms and Ammunition.

Henry Rifle.

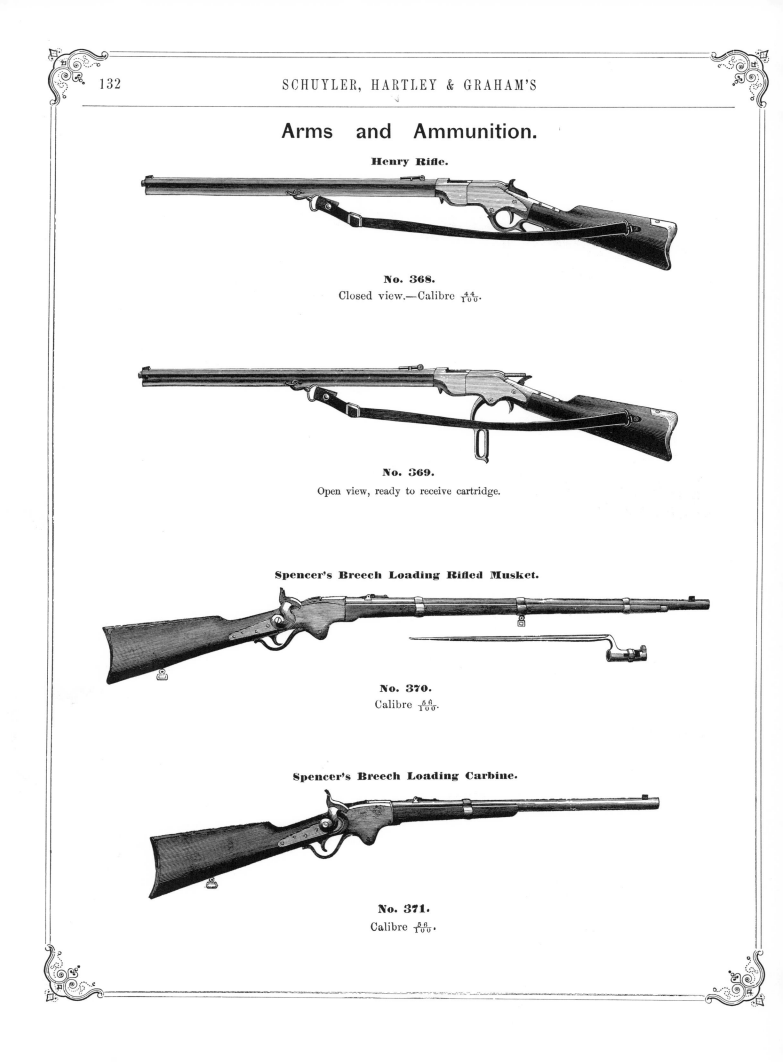

No. 368.

Closed view.—Calibre $\frac{44}{100}$.

No. 369.

Open view, ready to receive cartridge.

Spencer's Breech Loading Rifled Musket.

No. 370.

Calibre $\frac{56}{100}$.

Spencer's Breech Loading Carbine.

No. 371.

Calibre $\frac{56}{100}$.

Arms and Ammunition.

Smith's Patent Breech Loading Carbines and Rifles.

Military Carbine—Barrel 22 inches long, Weight 7½ pounds, Calibre 50–100ths of an inch.

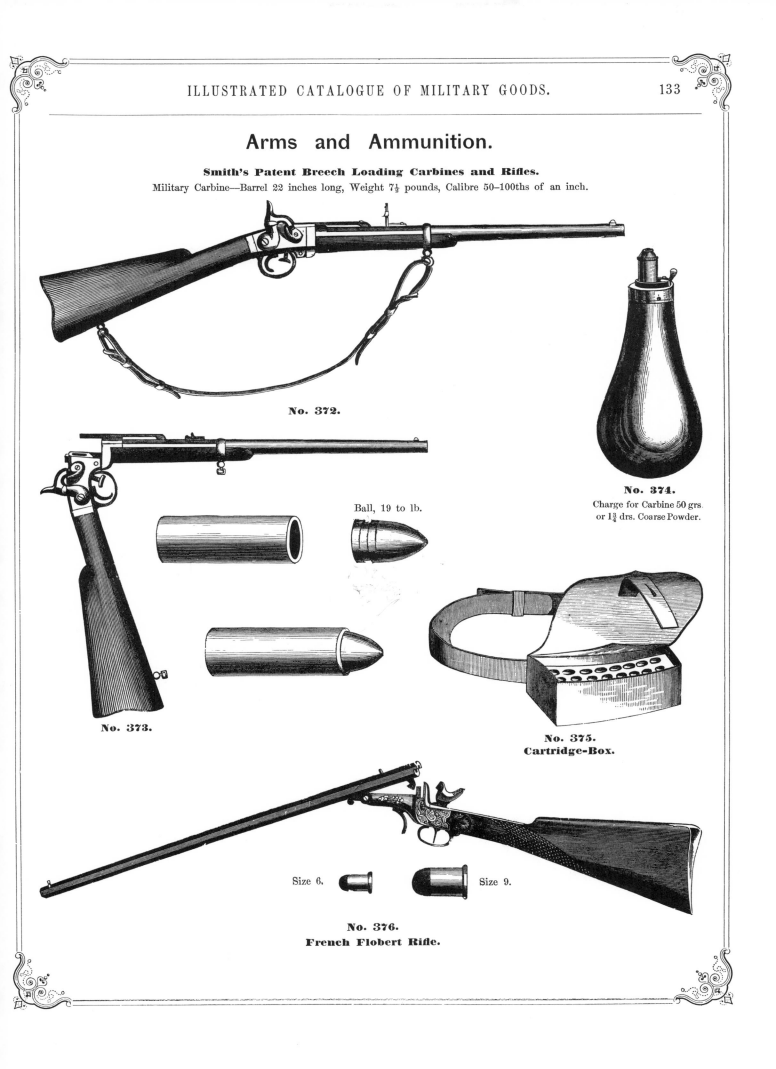

No. 372.

No. 374.

Charge for Carbine 50 grs.
or 1¾ drs. Coarse Powder.

Ball, 19 to lb.

No. 373.

No. 375.
Cartridge-Box.

Size 6.   Size 9.

No. 376.
French Flobert Rifle.

Arms and Ammunition.

Colt's Patent Rifles, Carbines and Shot Guns.

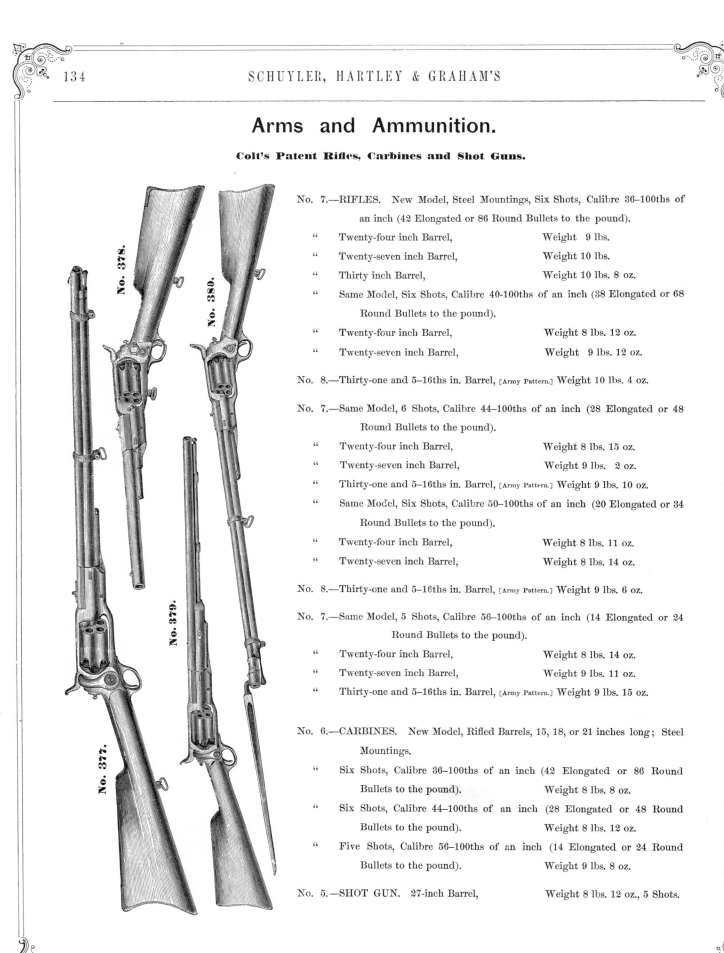

No. 378.

No. 380.

No. 379.

No. 377.

No. 7.—RIFLES. New Model, Steel Mountings, Six Shots, Calibre 36–100ths of an inch (42 Elongated or 86 Round Bullets to the pound).

" 　Twenty-four inch Barrel, 　　　　Weight　9 lbs.

" 　Twenty-seven inch Barrel, 　　　Weight 10 lbs.

" 　Thirty inch Barrel, 　　　　　　Weight 10 lbs. 8 oz.

" 　Same Model, Six Shots, Calibre 40-100ths of an inch (38 Elongated or 68 Round Bullets to the pound).

" 　Twenty-four inch Barrel, 　　　　Weight 8 lbs. 12 oz.

" 　Twenty-seven inch Barrel, 　　　Weight　9 lbs. 12 oz.

No. 8.—Thirty-one and 5–16ths in. Barrel, [Army Pattern.] Weight 10 lbs. 4 oz.

No. 7.—Same Model, 6 Shots, Calibre 44–100ths of an inch (28 Elongated or 48 Round Bullets to the pound).

" 　Twenty-four inch Barrel, 　　　　Weight 8 lbs. 15 oz.

" 　Twenty-seven inch Barrel, 　　　Weight 9 lbs.　2 oz.

" 　Thirty-one and 5–16ths in. Barrel, [Army Pattern.] Weight 9 lbs. 10 oz.

" 　Same Model, Six Shots, Calibre 50–100ths of an inch (20 Elongated or 34 Round Bullets to the pound).

" 　Twenty-four inch Barrel, 　　　　Weight 8 lbs. 11 oz.

" 　Twenty-seven inch Barrel, 　　　Weight 8 lbs. 14 oz.

No. 8.—Thirty-one and 5–16ths in. Barrel, [Army Pattern.] Weight 9 lbs. 6 oz.

No. 7.—Same Model, 5 Shots, Calibre 56–100ths of an inch (14 Elongated or 24 Round Bullets to the pound).

" 　Twenty-four inch Barrel, 　　　　Weight 8 lbs. 14 oz.

" 　Twenty-seven inch Barrel, 　　　Weight 9 lbs. 11 oz.

" 　Thirty-one and 5–16ths in. Barrel, [Army Pattern.] Weight 9 lbs. 15 oz.

No. 6.—CARBINES. New Model, Rifled Barrels, 15, 18, or 21 inches long; Steel Mountings.

" 　Six Shots, Calibre 36–100ths of an inch (42 Elongated or 86 Round Bullets to the pound). 　　Weight 8 lbs. 8 oz.

" 　Six Shots, Calibre 44–100ths of an inch (28 Elongated or 48 Round Bullets to the pound). 　　Weight 8 lbs. 12 oz.

" 　Five Shots, Calibre 56–100ths of an inch (14 Elongated or 24 Round Bullets to the pound). 　　Weight 9 lbs. 8 oz.

No. 5.—SHOT GUN. 27-inch Barrel, 　　　Weight 8 lbs. 12 oz., 5 Shots.

Arms and Ammunition.

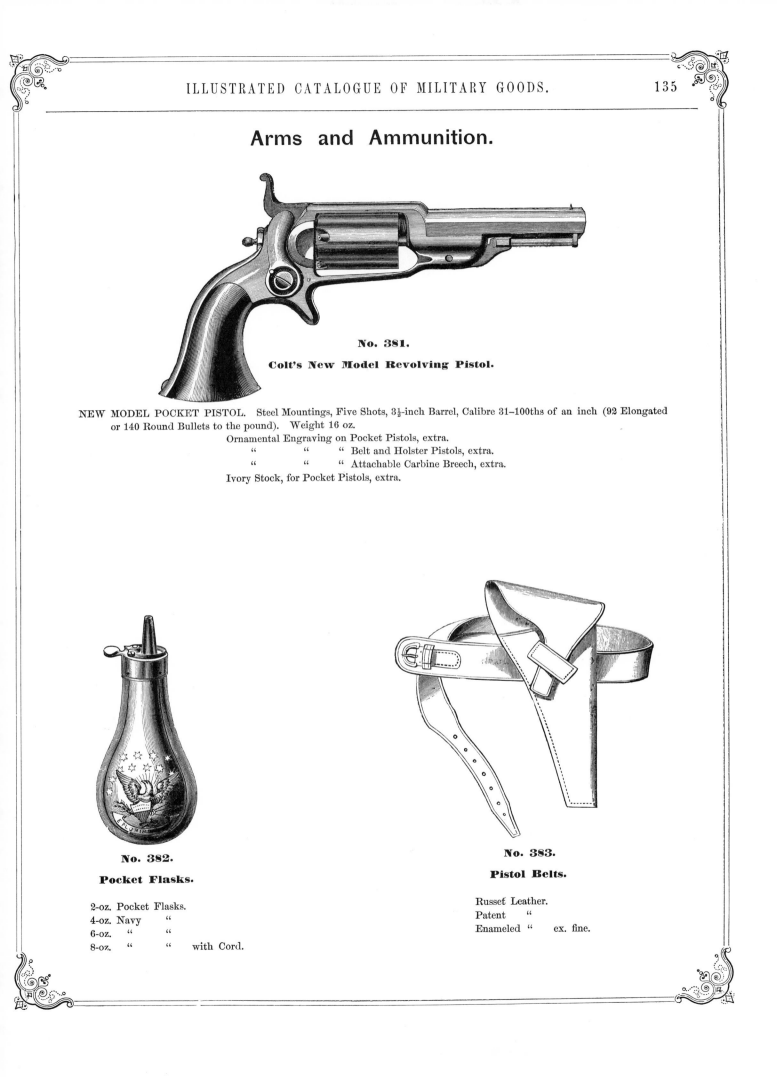

No. 381.

Colt's New Model Revolving Pistol.

NEW MODEL POCKET PISTOL.   Steel Mountings, Five Shots, 3½-inch Barrel, Calibre 31–100ths of an inch (92 Elongated or 140 Round Bullets to the pound).   Weight 16 oz.

Ornamental Engraving on Pocket Pistols, extra.

"   "   " Belt and Holster Pistols, extra.

"   "   " Attachable Carbine Breech, extra.

Ivory Stock, for Pocket Pistols, extra.

No. 382.

Pocket Flasks.

2-oz. Pocket Flasks.
4-oz. Navy   "
6-oz.   "   "
8-oz.   "   "   with Cord.

No. 383.

Pistol Belts.

Russet Leather.
Patent   "
Enameled "   ex. fine.

Arms and Ammunition.

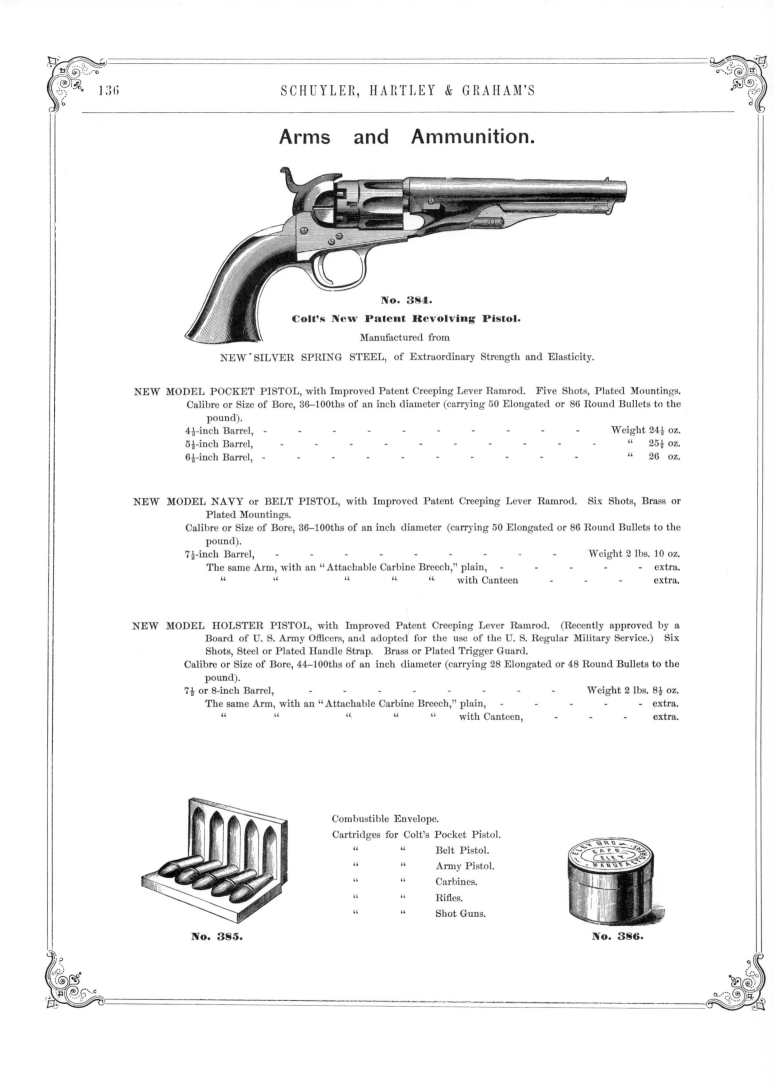

No. 384.
Colt's New Patent Revolving Pistol.
Manufactured from

NEW SILVER SPRING STEEL, of Extraordinary Strength and Elasticity.

NEW MODEL POCKET PISTOL, with Improved Patent Creeping Lever Ramrod. Five Shots, Plated Mountings.
Calibre or Size of Bore, 36–100ths of an inch diameter (carrying 50 Elongated or 86 Round Bullets to the pound).

4½-inch Barrel,	Weight 24½ oz.
5½-inch Barrel,	" 25½ oz.
6½-inch Barrel,	" 26 oz.

NEW MODEL NAVY or BELT PISTOL, with Improved Patent Creeping Lever Ramrod. Six Shots, Brass or Plated Mountings.
Calibre or Size of Bore, 36–100ths of an inch diameter (carrying 50 Elongated or 86 Round Bullets to the pound).

7½-inch Barrel,	Weight 2 lbs. 10 oz.
The same Arm, with an "Attachable Carbine Breech," plain,	extra.
" " " " " with Canteen	extra.

NEW MODEL HOLSTER PISTOL, with Improved Patent Creeping Lever Ramrod. (Recently approved by a Board of U. S. Army Officers, and adopted for the use of the U. S. Regular Military Service.) Six Shots, Steel or Plated Handle Strap. Brass or Plated Trigger Guard.
Calibre or Size of Bore, 44–100ths of an inch diameter (carrying 28 Elongated or 48 Round Bullets to the pound).

7½ or 8-inch Barrel,	Weight 2 lbs. 8½ oz.
The same Arm, with an "Attachable Carbine Breech," plain,	extra.
" " " " " with Canteen,	extra.

Combustible Envelope.
Cartridges for Colt's Pocket Pistol.

"	"	Belt Pistol.
"	"	Army Pistol.
"	"	Carbines.
"	"	Rifles.
"	"	Shot Guns.

No. 385.   **No. 386.**

Arms and Ammunition.

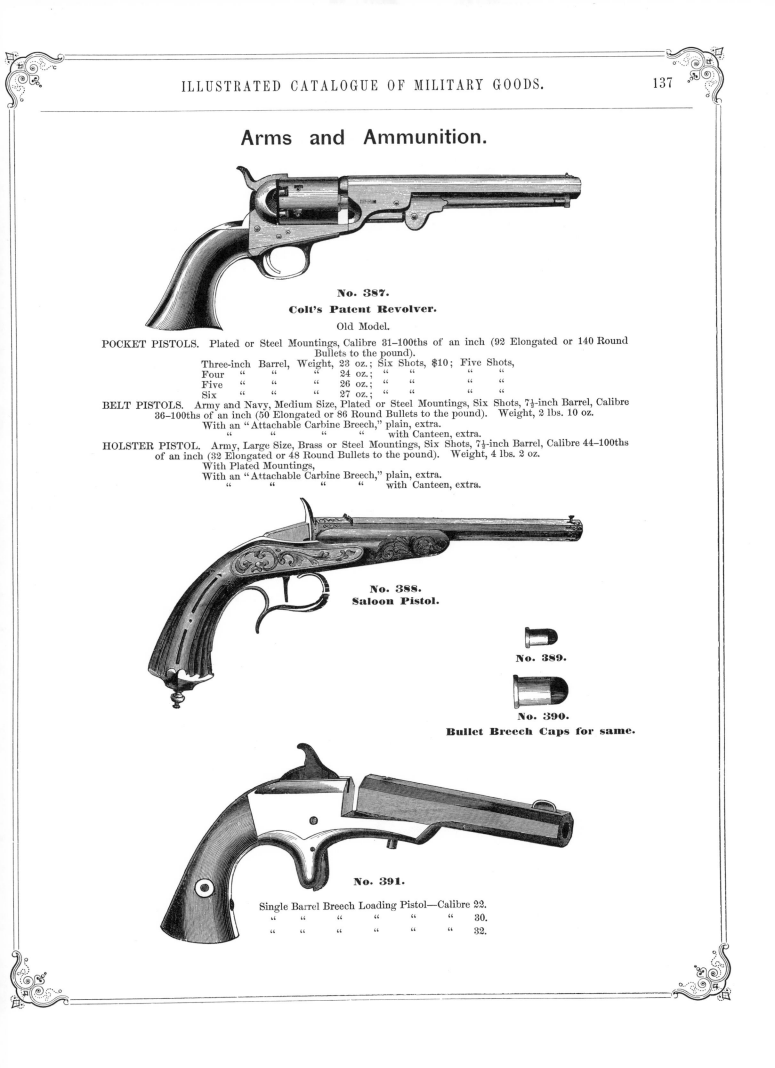

No. 387.

Colt's Patent Revolver.

Old Model.

POCKET PISTOLS. Plated or Steel Mountings, Calibre 31–100ths of an inch (92 Elongated or 140 Round Bullets to the pound).

Three-inch Barrel, Weight, 23 oz.; Six Shots, $10; Five Shots,
Four   "   "   " 24 oz.; "   "   "   "
Five   "   "   " 26 oz.; "   "   "   "
Six   "   "   " 27 oz.; "   "   "   "

BELT PISTOLS. Army and Navy, Medium Size, Plated or Steel Mountings, Six Shots, 7½-inch Barrel, Calibre 36–100ths of an inch (50 Elongated or 86 Round Bullets to the pound).   Weight, 2 lbs. 10 oz.
With an "Attachable Carbine Breech," plain, extra.
"   "   "   "   " with Canteen, extra.

HOLSTER PISTOL. Army, Large Size, Brass or Steel Mountings, Six Shots, 7½-inch Barrel, Calibre 44–100ths of an inch (32 Elongated or 48 Round Bullets to the pound).   Weight, 4 lbs. 2 oz.
With Plated Mountings,
With an "Attachable Carbine Breech," plain, extra.
"   "   "   "   " with Canteen, extra.

No. 388.
Saloon Pistol.

No. 389.

No. 390.

Bullet Breech Caps for same.

No. 391.

Single Barrel Breech Loading Pistol—Calibre 22.
"   "   "   "   "   " 30.
"   "   "   "   "   " 32.

Arms and Ammunition.

Smith & Wesson's Breech Loading Pistols, with Cylinder detached.

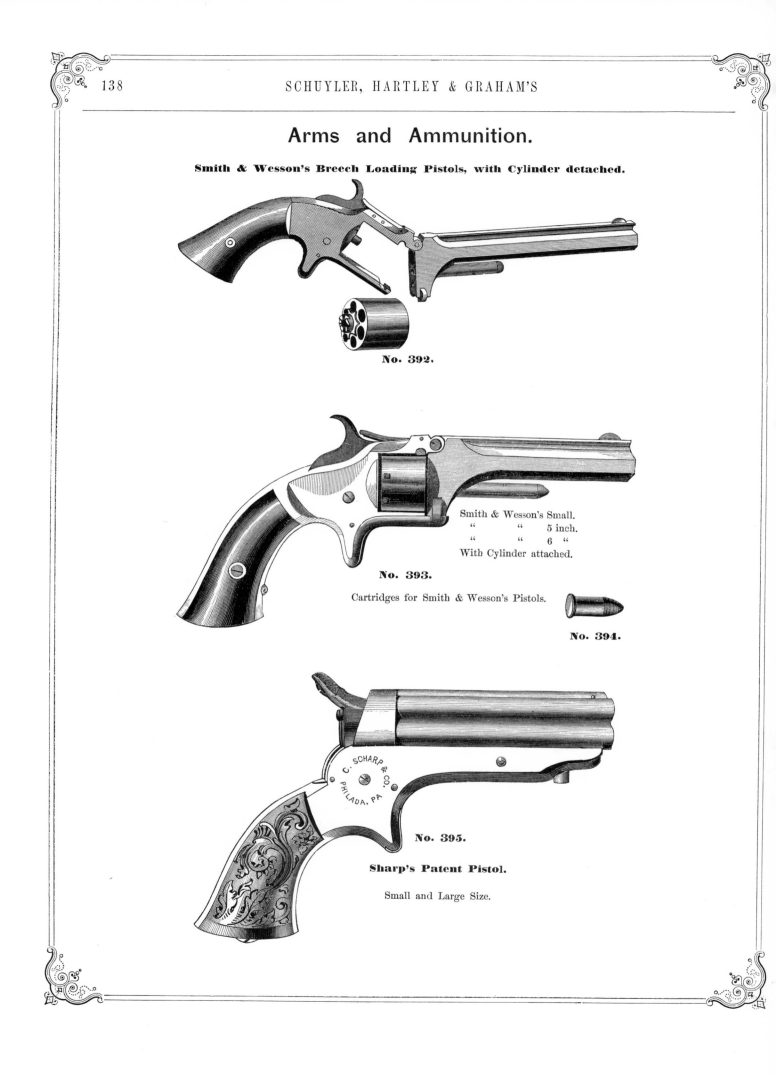

No. 392.

Smith & Wesson's Small.
"   "   5 inch.
"   "   6 "
With Cylinder attached.

No. 393.

Cartridges for Smith & Wesson's Pistols.

No. 394.

No. 395.

Sharp's Patent Pistol.

Small and Large Size.

Arms and Ammunition.

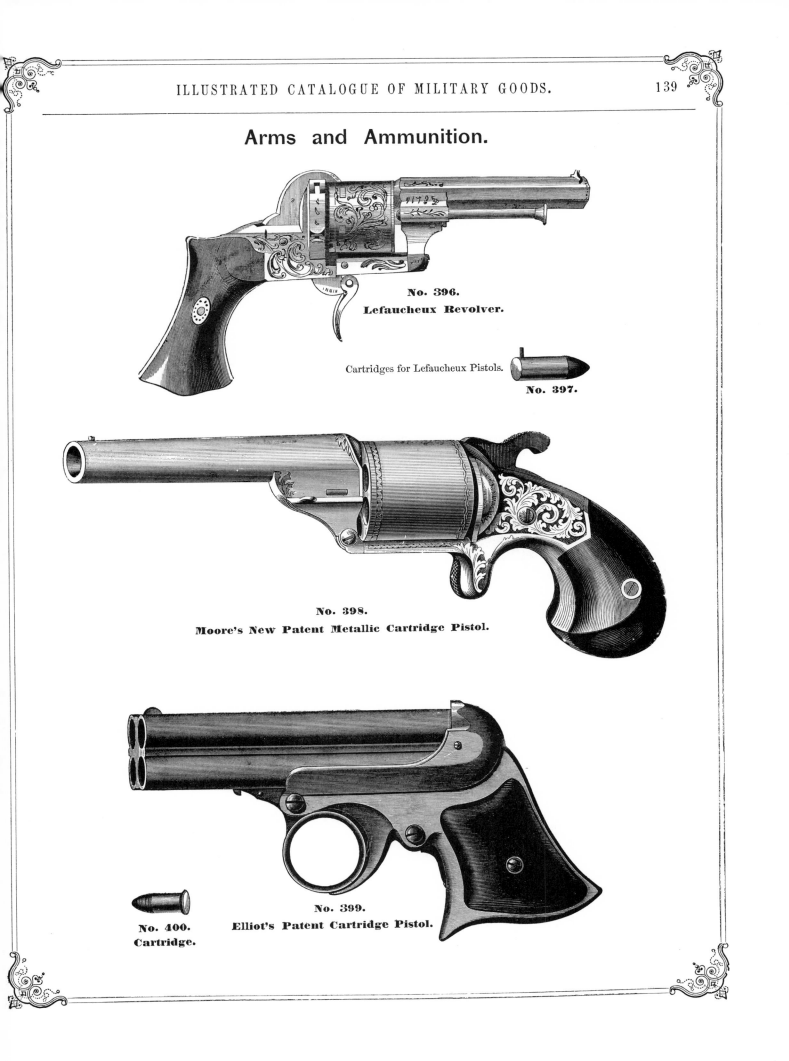

No. 396.
Lefaucheux Revolver.

Cartridges for Lefaucheux Pistols.

No. 397.

No. 398.
Moore's New Patent Metallic Cartridge Pistol.

No. 400.
Cartridge.

No. 399.
Elliot's Patent Cartridge Pistol.

Arms and Ammunition.

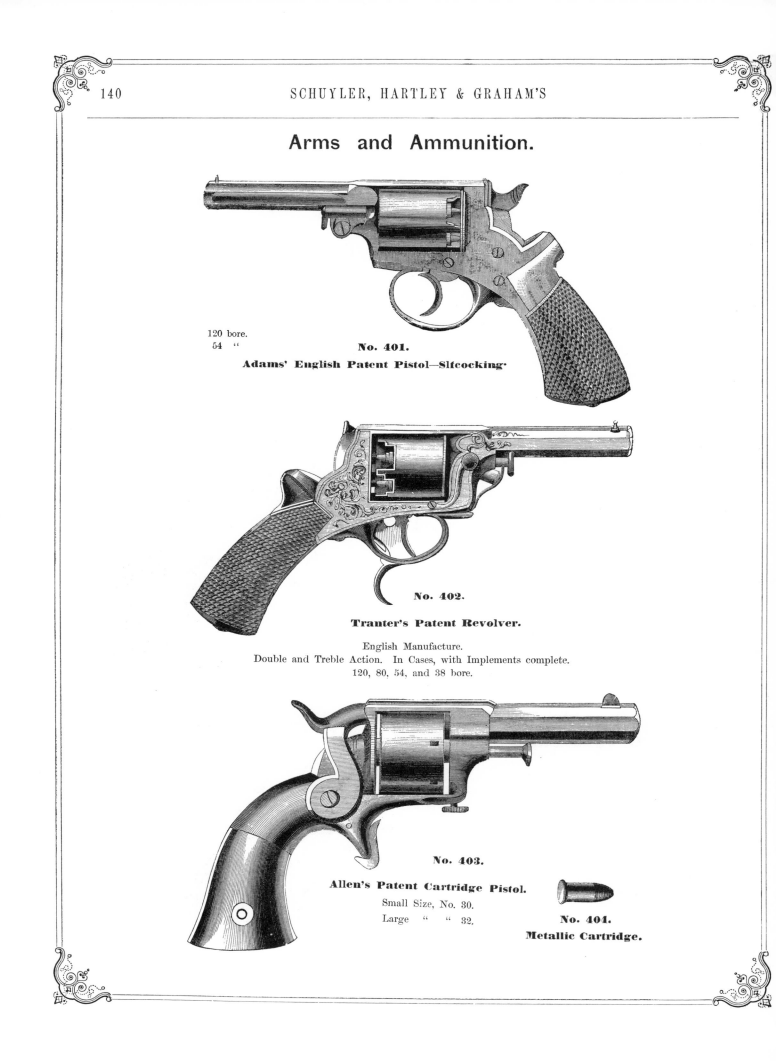

120 bore.
54 "

No. 401.

Adams' English Patent Pistol—Sltcocking·

No. 402.

Tranter's Patent Revolver.

English Manufacture.
Double and Treble Action. In Cases, with Implements complete.
120, 80, 54, and 38 bore.

No. 403.

Allen's Patent Cartridge Pistol.

Small Size, No. 30.
Large " " 32.

No. 404.

Metallic Cartridge.

Arms and Ammunition.

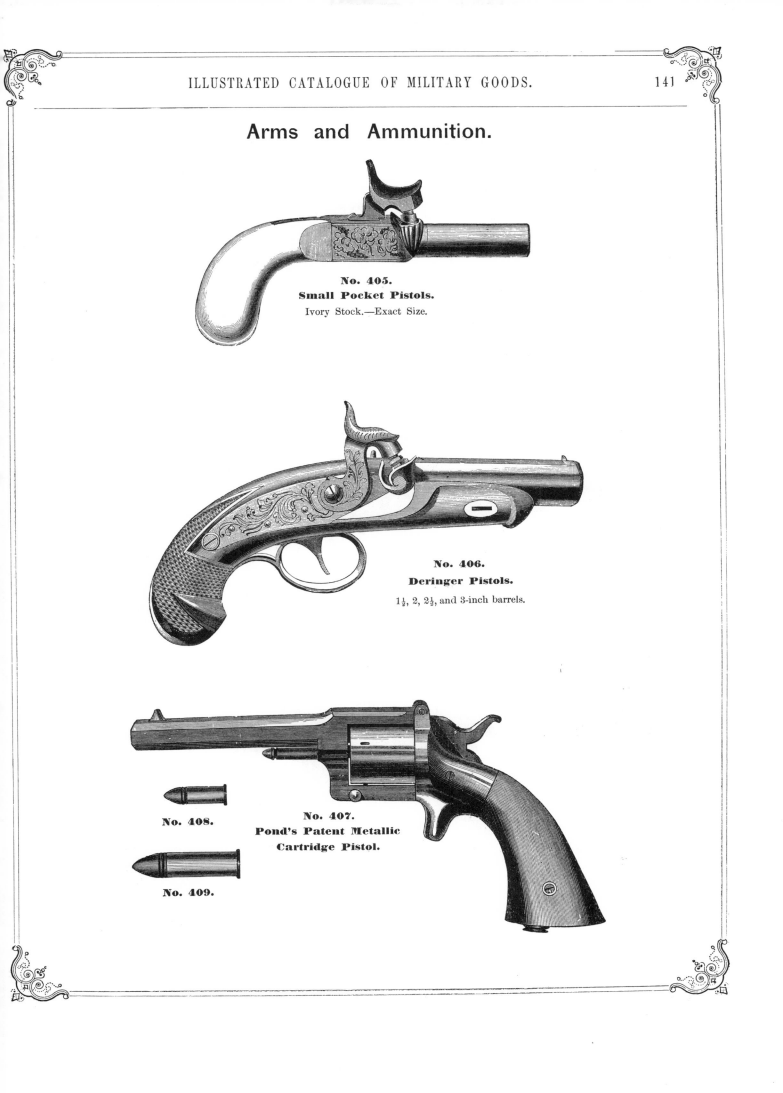

No. 405.
Small Pocket Pistols.
Ivory Stock.—Exact Size.

No. 406.
Deringer Pistols.
1½, 2, 2½, and 3-inch barrels.

No. 408.

No. 409.

No. 407.
Pond's Patent Metallic
Cartridge Pistol.

Arms and Ammunition.

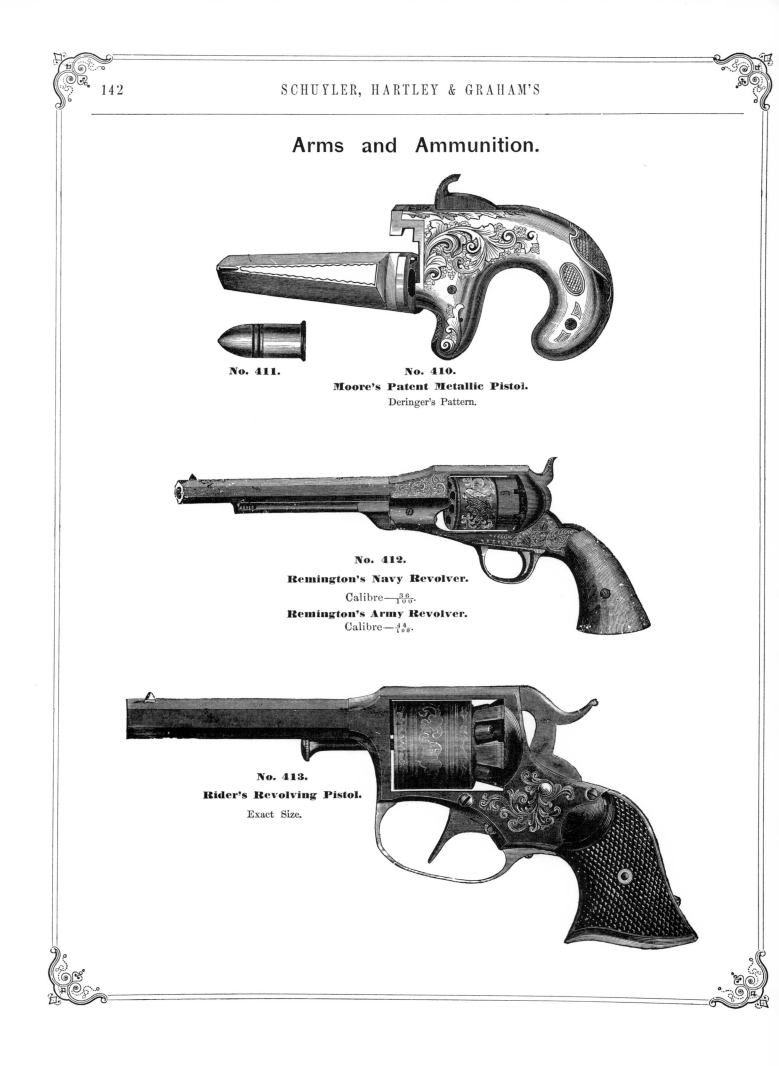

No. 411.   **No. 410.**

Moore's Patent Metallic Pistol.

Deringer's Pattern.

No. 412.

Remington's Navy Revolver.

Calibre—$\frac{36}{100}$.

Remington's Army Revolver.

Calibre—$\frac{44}{100}$.

No. 413.

Rider's Revolving Pistol.

Exact Size.

COATS OF ARMS.

UNITED STATES.

MAINE.

NEW HAMPSHIRE.

VERMONT.

MASSACHUSETTS.

RHODE ISLAND.

CONNECTICUT.

NEW YORK.

PENNSYLVANIA.

NEW JERSEY.

DELAWARE.

MARYLAND.

OHIO.

INDIANA.

MICHIGAN

ILLINOIS.

WISCONSIN.

MINNESOTA.

IOWA

MISSOURI.

KENTUCKY.

KANSAS.

VIRGINIA.

NORTH CAROLINA.

SOUTH CAROLINA.

GEORGIA.

FLORIDA.

ALABAMA.

LOUISIANA.

TEXAS.

MISSISSIPPI.

ARKANSAS.

TENNESSEE.

CALIFORNIA.

OREGON.